FRONTIERS OF DANCE

The Life of Martha Graham

FRONTIERS OF DANCE

The Life of Martha Graham

by Walter Terry

illustrated with photographs

Thomas Y. Crowell Company   New York

The author and the publisher are grateful to Martha Graham for permission to use the photographs on pages 6, 12, 25, and 84. Illustrations on pages 19, 31, 33, 36, 41, 46, 50, 55, 118, and 130 are from the collection of Walter Terry.

Library of Congress Cataloging in Publication Data
Terry, Walter.   Frontiers of dance.
(Women of America series)
Bibliography: p. / Includes index.
Summary: A biography of the dancer, choreographer,
and teacher who is generally considered to be one of
America's greatest pioneers of modern dance.
1. Graham, Martha—Juv. lit.   2. Modern dance—Juv. lit.
[1. Graham, Martha.   2. Dancers.   3. Modern dance—Biography]
I. Title. GV1785.G7T47   [793.3'092'4]   [B]   [92]   75-9871
ISBN 0–690–00920–8

1 2 3 4 5 6 7 8 9 10

To Carolyn

Who urges me ever so gently—
but firmly!—to put down on paper
what I talk about all the time:
DANCE AND DANCERS

WOMEN OF AMERICA
Milton Meltzer, EDITOR

Contents

Illustrations

Foreword

I revere Martha Graham as a great artist and a great woman. I cherish Martha Graham as a very dear friend.

I first saw her dance in 1932, and I didn't like her very much, mainly because I was not prepared to respond to what was then a very new approach to the ancient art of dancing. I first met her in 1936; it was the first interview I ever did as a professional newspaper writer. Right then and there I hoped that we would become friends, although I was very young and she had been a dancer for twenty years.

And we did become friends. We have talked and agreed and argued and laughed. We have dined alone.

I have cooked dinner for her and she has made scrambled eggs for me. Almost always we have talked about dance, but when I've had personal problems, she has listened and been both loving and helpful. I think—I hope—I have occasionally done the same for her.

This book, then, contains not only the facts of the remarkable career of Martha Graham but many of my own personal visits with her, talks with her, and experiences with her. Indeed, forty years of friendship with Martha Graham constitute an essential part of this report on a great woman of the dance.

W. T.

FRONTIERS OF DANCE

Prologue

The Curtain Rises

"Martha," said Dr. Graham, "you are not telling the truth. Don't you know when you do something like this I always know? There is always some movement that tells me you are deceiving me. You see, no matter what you say, you reveal yourself—you make fists you think I don't notice, your back gets very straight, maybe you shuffle your feet, your eyelids drop. Movement does not lie." To the wide-eyed five-year-old girl in the Pittsburgh suburb of Allegheny, it was terrifying to be caught in a lie.

In the Presbyterian church, which her family attended, one of the first things she had learned was that lying was a sin. Looking up into her father's face,

Martha shuddered as he said, "You always reveal yourself to me through movement." Looking back seventy-five years later, she said, "In a way, this was my very first dancing lesson."

The average little girl's first dancing lesson is that exciting occasion when her mother takes her to a ballet, tap, or modern dance class or when, after school, she learns the steps and the patterns of social and folk dancing. For ballet, she puts on leotard and tights or maybe just a bathing suit, and she has soft ballet slippers on her feet, although she probably dreams of the day when her teacher will permit her to put on toe shoes and rise onto *pointe*, onto the tips of her toes like the ballerinas she has seen in the theater or on television.

But Martha Graham's first lesson was different. She was not learning about steps or ballroom figures or whether to count one-two-three or one-two-three-four. She was learning, although she didn't know it at the time, about a new way of dance that would change not only her life but the whole theater of dance around the world.

Her first teacher was neither a retired ballerina nor a physical education instructor. It was her father, a family doctor who took care of mumps and measles, pneumonia, childbirth—the beginnings of life, the fare-wells of dying. He was a doctor who was experimenting with psychology. Dr. Graham taught his oldest daughter that movements did not lie. In the long years ahead, however she may have dissembled offstage, Martha never told a lie with her body onstage. Hers was to be the theater of revelation, of truth.

The Journey Begins

The biography of a dancer can be like that of no other human. We are always curious about how someone looked as a child, where and when someone was born, bits of family history. But a dancer's art, unlike that of a doctor with his medicines and surgical instruments or a musician with a violin or a piano or an artist with paints and brushes, is almost self-contained. The dancer's body itself is the tool. The dancer's art begins and ends with the body, just as movement dies in the fraction in which it lives. It is of the instant.

You may say, "Well, yes, but the dancer is no different from the athlete, whose body is his instrument." But there is a difference. Martha Graham has

3

called dancers "divine athletes," for not only is the body
the dancer's instrument, it is also the house in which
dwell the emotions, the passions, sometimes the ecstasies
which must be expressed through mute, but eloquent,
movement.

Who *is* Martha Graham? She is a tiny, exotic-look-
ing woman, whose face, with its high cheekbones and
large mouth, suggests a primitive mask. But what lies
behind that mask? Where, indeed, does the true biography exist?

Martha Graham often uses the phrase "interior
landscape" to describe her purpose and her method in
creating characters for the stage. This great dancer, one
of the greatest of all time, cannot be truly revealed in a
biography that would be content with photographing
the exterior "landscape" of a little girl as she stands
before her father, goes to school, is put in a corner
because she has been naughty, or, as a young lady, bows
graciously to guests. No, we must get to that "interior"
landscape that shows us how she feels when she stands
before her father, what her conscience says to her when
she has been naughty, what passes through her mind
when she is polite to guests although fear or fury may
possess her heart.

This "interior landscape" is everyone's true, and
perhaps secret, biography. It is especially important for
the dancer. It is absolutely essential in the case of
Martha Graham. How else can we understand what
motivated her to sweat and ache and hurt, to drive her
muscles, tendons, ligaments, joints, and the flesh itself
remorselessly day after day for a lifetime, to become a
divine athlete, able to reveal the interior landscapes of
history's heroines through the dances she created for the
world's theater.

The exterior landscape that was the scene of Martha Graham's birth on May 11, 1894, was the community of Allegheny, Pennsylvania, in the Pittsburgh area. Martha was to find dance inspiration in the Orient, in ancient Greece, and in other remote places and times. But fifty years after her birth, she would choreograph a journey to the Allegheny Mountains and to the majestic Appalachian Mountain system of which they are a part, to create her most famous dance, her testament both to America and to her own American heritage, *Appalachian Spring.*

In Allegheny, when Martha was born, the days of the pioneers were already a part of history. But the echoes were still there. Both her parents had been born in Allegheny country, only a generation or two removed from those who had trekked west from the seacoast to Indian land, to virgin territory. It was inevitable that *Appalachian Spring* and her most famous solo, *Frontier*, would one day spring from her ancient heritage to the stages of the world.

Martha's mother was Jane Beers, always known as Jenny, and through her, Martha traced her ancestry right back to Miles Standish and the first settlers who arrived on the *Mayflower*. Her father, George Graham, was the grandson of an immigrant who had, in the words of his great-granddaughter, "more than a touch of Black Irish in him." Martha proved to be an even mixture of the two strains, a stern, indomitable, God-fearing Puritan pioneer on one side and on the other a wild, tempestuous, moody, dream-obsessed, and quick-to-anger creature of the "Black Irish" persuasion.

These two strains seem to be in violent conflict, and indeed they are. In Martha's case they produced an individual unlike anyone else in the world. In later

Martha Graham, about two years old.

George and Jenny Graham, father and mother.

years she would look a student in the eye when doubts were expressed about his or her special gifts, and say, "Only *you* were born at an exact moment to the same parents and the same grandparents and the same set of ancestors in exactly the same bed in the same spot in the same room in the same house in the same time. The combination has never happened before and it will never happen again. You are, therefore, unique." Martha was unique.

Environment, as well as ancestry, affects a being. Martha was born in that period which we now look back on as the Victorian Age. The British Queen who gave her name to the era also impressed her moral standards upon it. Queen Victoria, who reigned for more than sixty years, was stern, proper, devoted to family life, disapproving of gaiety, and a champion of duty. Victoria's influence spread to Allegheny, Pennsylvania.

Martha and her two younger sisters, Mary and Georgia (always known as Geordie or Jeordie), had a strict upbringing. The distant Victoria and the still more distant Puritan ancestors saw to that. Not only Sunday school and church attendance, but daily prayers were required. Many years later Martha used her austere grandmother as the model for the forbidding Ancestress in her dance of the New England poet Emily Dickinson, *Letter to the World*. In a scene in which the dancer kneels and peers through the slats of a chair, there is the memory of herself as a little girl, kneeling in prayer in the family parlor and peeking at the other worshippers.

The little Graham sisters—a brother had died shortly after birth—made their own world in their own house. This was partly due to the protectiveness of Victorians for their womenfolk and partly, as Martha recalls, because "like all doctors' children we were sick with colds and sniffles, so we made a sort of theater at home." Mrs. Graham, herself a doll-like figure (Dr. Graham liked to pick up his wife and carry her about as if she were indeed a fragile doll), made dress-up clothes for the girls.

Martha, as the oldest (Mary was two years younger and Jeordie six) and the most adventuresome, was the ringleader. "I was a very difficult child," she recalls with a sly smile indicating understatement. Indeed, she was always getting into trouble and torn between lying about it (and the awful Presbyterian consequences) and telling the truth and accepting her punishment on earth. Her mother discovered that she was less likely to get into trouble if she was encouraged in "pretending" and making a theater in her own home.

She made up the stories and told her sisters what to do and when to do it. Woebetide anyone who crossed her, for not only was she "difficult," but she had a fiery temper that was almost destructive, a temper that never faded. Her old-time friends and her newest associates know the warning signs: the lips pulled back from the big and gleaming teeth in something not too far removed from the snarl of a tigress. A wise person could sense that she was about to strike. Her sisters and, later, her schoolmates learned to recognize the sign and to get out of the way. Yet Martha was genuinely kind and tender (when not crossed) and surprisingly sentimental. Another strange contrast was that she was a very plain child and teen-ager, and yet she recalls that she was "inordinately vain." By dressing up, by pretending to be someone else, she escaped her own plainness. This proved to be true of her until middle age, when she created an offstage glamour equal to her hypnotic stage presences.

At first, in her childhood games, there was no dancing at all. Hymns in church made her want to move about rhythmically, and there is a legend that once she actually danced up and down the aisles of the Presbyterian church until she was quickly brought to order. Little Martha did not see anything resembling real theater until her parents took her to a Punch and Judy show in Atlantic City. She was so tiny that her legs stuck straight out in front of her as she sat motionless, but enthralled, in an adult-size theater chair.

But once again, she learned more about the nature of movement from her father than she did from any other source. She listened, at mealtimes, to her father talking about his patients to Mrs. Graham. Martha was quiet, she asked no questions, but she was all ears as Dr. Graham discussed with his wife the motions of patients, movements that seemed strange, not quite ordinary. And he would say what these movements, both voluntary and involuntary, revealed.

Dr. Graham, after he had graduated from Johns Hopkins, had begun his practice at Dixmont, a home for the mentally disturbed, which his father had established outside Pittsburgh. During the day, as a specialist in mental health—in that era he was termed an "alienist" rather than a "psychologist"—he doctored his patients, but in the evening he would often entertain them by playing songs from Gilbert and Sullivan operettas, Viennese waltzes, and all kinds of romantic tunes on the piano. He was a charming, debonair gentleman and enormously popular with the patients. The worst punishment that could be given them for bad behavior was to be banned from Dr. Graham's evening recitals.

Dr. Graham favored romantic music, lovely ladies, and especially his wife. Nothing pleased him more than to pamper her, to shower her with presents. Her most casual comment would give him an excuse to buy her a gift, such as a bantam hen and her tiny chicks, which Mrs. Graham had noticed in a shopwindow at Eastertime. But if he treated her as a toy, as gentlemen of culture tended to treat their wives in the 1890s, he also respected her mind. It was for this reason that he confided in her his observations on the behavior of his Dixmont patients.

Martha was much too young to know what he meant by all his comments. She was simply aware that he understood what his patients were thinking and feeling, just as he could tell whether or not she was fibbing by the way she moved. It all seemed very logical. She listened, learned, and stored it all away in her mind until, thinking back at an older age, she was able to sort it out and apply it to her own search for the theater of truth.

In school she was a quick learner. In fact, she mastered her lessons so easily that her teachers were somewhat at a loss to keep her occupied. The easiest thing to do was to send her off to the library with the instruction: "Look at some books."

Martha did more than look. Although she was only a child, picture books held little interest for her. She read. She read about people. She learned of heroes and heroines, of goddesses, of kings and queens, of warriors.

It didn't much matter *whom* she happened to read about, it was *what* they were like inside that fascinated her, and how they faced the joys and crises of their lives. Indeed, from the very beginning of her reading, Martha found herself hypnotized by the drama of life. She did not, even at ten or twelve years old, identify herself with theater, only with the mystery of people. She herself was mysterious. Her violent temper was a clear response to not getting her own way. If someone addressed her when she was in a mood of retirement or reverie or some profound thought process, she would remain silent, her face like a mask. In this, she was quite unlike her pretty, seemingly delicate little mother, who concealed an iron will beneath the sweetest and most obedient of smiles. She was more like her father with his quick temper and his contrasting quiet curiosity as he studied the mysteries of various personalities.

There was also, beneath the mask-like face, something of that adventuresome grandfather whose deep concern for the insane and the emotionally unstable had caused him to establish Dixmont. And perhaps too something of that great-grandfather who had arrived in the New World from Europe with just enough money for either bed or breakfast and who had chosen the bed because he was confident that he could earn his breakfast. (He not only earned that breakfast but subsequently enough money to open the first bank in Pittsburgh.)

Another major influence was Lizzie. Elizabeth Pendergast had been a patient of Dr. Graham's. She was devoted to him, and when Martha was born, Lizzie trotted over to the Graham home, knocked on the door, and told young Mrs. Graham, "You'll be needing me."

Martha and her younger sister, Mary, with their nurse Lizzie Pendergast.

She never left. Whether the family adopted her or she adopted the Grahams didn't matter much. Lizzie became a fixture. She was Irish, talkative, filled with fancies and fantasies, and adored helping Martha and her two sisters to make their costumes for the world of make-believe that was as real to Lizzie as the practical world in which she had been set down.

In due course, Lizzie, with no intent to work a religious conversion, exposed Martha to her own Catholicism. The child responded instantly to the music and rituals of the Roman church, for it was in distinct contrast to the austere Presbyterian prayers and services in which she was officially being reared. Dr. Graham did not object to what Lizzie was doing. Indeed, he and his brothers, as youngsters, had been sent to the nearest church school in the hope that its guidance would give them a discipline that they failed to find in the public school. Dr. Graham, though remaining a Presbyterian, never forgot, as he put it, "the music and the costumes of the Catholic Church" that had so attracted him as a child.

Mrs. Graham was equally tolerant. She made no effort to stamp out her daughter's fascination with the striking ceremonies of Lizzie's church.

When Martha entered her teens, another major event occurred which was to have a profound, even fateful, influence on her. Her sister Mary had always been bothered with asthma, and as she was growing up, the attacks became increasingly serious. Dr. Graham felt that a complete change of climate was essential to his daughter's health, so he set out for California to find the place that would be most beneficial to the child. He settled on Santa Barbara, a seacoast city slightly north of Los Angeles, noted for its warm, fresh, and pure air. In 1908 he moved his family there. He himself, because of his responsibilities at Dixmont, could not move with them. He visited them whenever he could until 1912, when he was able to come to Santa Barbara for what were to be his few remaining years.

The Grahams, Martha especially, took to Santa Barbara instantly and to a wholly new way of life in wholly new surroundings. The Graham girls had never seen Orientals before, and in California the servants were invariably Oriental, bringing their own ways to the households in which they worked. Martha never forgot her enchantment with the contrast between the cool, unemotional sternness of the people in the Presbyterian community in Allegheny and "the gentle, mystical, beauty-loving characteristics of these new people in a new climate."

The individual, of course, is molded both by his heritage and his environment. At fourteen, Martha had not yet been exposed to dance, and no one, least of all Martha herself, would have guessed that buried in this small, homely child, this "bookworm," was the seed that was to flower into one of the towering dance figures of the twentieth century. She had not yet learned or even made up a dance step, but the core of her theater of dance was already present. Only the disciplines—the training, the technique—of the dancer were missing. Can we see, then, what heralded the career?

The kind of dance that Martha would create had its roots in the rituals of the Catholic Church and the ceremony of manners that she found in the Orientals in California. These influences supplied the exterior, perhaps we could call it the architecture, of her later dances. And for necessary dramatic conflict within these rituals, she would summon up her own Puritan heritage, with its severe restraints and its terror of wrongdoing.

As a teen-ager, Martha's mind did not dwell on such matters; it simply stored them away. In high school, she studied, continued to read, and had a go at writing. She became editor of *Olive and Gold*, the literary magazine of the Santa Barbara High School. She acted the role of Dido in a play based upon *The Aeneid* of the great Latin poet Vergil. She played basketball. And she had a perfectly normal social life, for if she was not pretty, she was vain about her mind, her acting skills, and a personality that she felt was different and effective. She liked boys, and she loved parties and going to school dances. Her first beau, John, later became an army officer. "I thought he was super!" Martha remembered years later.

But there were restrictions of a sort. Although she loved the school dances and was permitted to attend them, she was not allowed to go to dancing school. This ban was not imposed because of any belief on the part of her parents that dancing was a sin. It was simply regarded as a minor diversion; Dr. and Mrs. Graham felt that dancing lessons should not interfere with school lessons. Education came first. Homework had to be done before she could go to a dance. And if the dance took place on a Saturday night, she must be home and in bed by midnight because, one minute later, it would be the Sabbath.

Martha was an unusual girl in ordinary surroundings. The unusual in her—the fantasies, the dreams of theater, the curiosity about what people were really like deep inside, the fascination with ritual wherever she found it—all came together in an experience that changed her life. For in 1911 she saw her first dancer. It happened to be one of the great dancers of the age. Not a classical ballerina, not a European star, but an American woman who had discovered a new approach to dance, one that combined the Oriental ceremony that young Martha adored with an acute understanding of people.

The dancer was Ruth St. Denis.

The Goddess

She first saw her on a poster. Pictured on it was an exceptionally beautiful woman in Oriental dress. It wasn't the sort of dress that Chinese servants wore. This woman looked more like a goddess, tall, regal, glittering, her eyes half-lowered as if she were partly concealing, partly revealing a mystery. Ruth St. Denis, the poster announced, would appear in a program of four solos from her spectacle *Egypta*, and in *The Five East Indian Dances*. April 24–29, 1911, was the time, and the Los Angeles Mason Opera House, the place.

Martha pleaded with her father to take her to Los Angeles. Since he made frequent trips to the city, he agreed to indulge his daughter. Indeed, he turned it into an occasion and gave Martha a little bouquet of violets, the first corsage she had ever received.

When the curtain rose in the opera house and revealed the poster-goddess in the flesh, it was all settled in Martha's mind. She said later, "From that moment on my fate was sealed. I couldn't wait to learn to dance as the goddess danced."

Martha had known nothing at all about St. Denis before she had seen the poster. In fact, she knew of no kind of dancing except the social dances at the high school proms. Perhaps in her reading she had come across references to classical ballet, but ballet had almost disappeared in America in the latter half of the nineteenth century. When Martha saw St. Denis, the great Russian ballerina Anna Pavlova had just made her first immense impact in distant New York.

Although she had had no exposure to theater dance before, Martha not only responded instantly to the St. Denis magic, she was actually able to remember some of the dances and what they were like. The *Egypta* excerpts seemed not to have made a major impression on her, although in later years she would find herself drawn to the art and the mysteries of ancient Egypt, even to the point of half-believing that she had been an Egyptian in an earlier incarnation. But it was St. Denis's dances of India that made indelible impressions on her mind.

She remembered *The Incense.* It is not quite dawn. Stepping through an opening in the *purdah,* the great veil that screens the women of the household from the eyes of men, comes a woman. She is wrapped in a *sari,* the traditional yards-upon-yards of material exquisitely draped about her body. In her hands is a tray of

The "Goddess"—Ruth St. Denis.   SOICHI SUNAMI

incense, its wisps of smoke curling upward. With her fingers, she crumbles bits of incense into the charcoal embers on the tray to enlarge the columns of smoke, and she moves to braziers elsewhere in the room to add incense to their coals. She sets down her tray and her arms begin a ripple that rises upward as if mirroring the rise of the smoke. The incense is used in prayers. The woman, by making her body become a part of the pattern of incense, becomes a living embodiment of prayer. This is the mother asking the gods to bless her household, her family, her home as a new day dawns.

She remembered *The Cobras*. Here too those wonderfully mobile arms moved as if they had no bones at all. But the gentleness of incense smoke was not in them in this dance. They became writhing snakes attached to the body of a filthy beggar. St. Denis, with two green-stone rings on each hand, suggesting the glittering, evil eyes of the cobras, used her arms to coil, dart, shift, poise, and strike with frightening effect. At the close of the dance, set in a corner of a street bazaar, the beggar calls for *"Baksheesh!"*—alms—and when she doesn't get any coins from the passersby she curses them, spits, tosses her snakes over her shoulders and exits. The cobra heads with their fiercely glaring eyes are the last view of the beggar.

The Yogi. St. Denis as a Hindu holy man, a man possessed of inner ecstasy yet utterly serene. He walks through an imaginary forest with great strides, head lifted to the heavens. He is on a mission of spiritual purpose. But for the yogi, repose, contemplation are essential to his discipline, to the renewal of his spirit. He stands on one foot and bends his body in the four directions of the compass. Then he sits, cross-legged, in a position that is called "the lotus seat." He lowers his eyes, and his arms move in the yoga exercises of breathing, holding the spine erect, moving the arms in patterns that seem to push aside the tawdriness of the world. His silent prayer finished, his eyes open wide, he rises and strides forth to bring his message of the spirit to others.

Radha. It is a temple scene. A goddess sits upon a dais. The lights are low and only a shaft of pale blue light falls from above directly upon the statue, a statue of bronze. But is it a statue? Priests enter to pay homage, and such is their faith that the goddess's lowered lids lift slowly and her eyes look out into infinity. An unseen breath swells her bosom and the statue takes on the movements of the living.

The goddess Radha does not speak in words. Her sermon to her followers is in gesture and in dance. She reminds them of the earthly delights of the five human senses of sight, smell, hearing, taste, and touch. Her eyes shine as she fondles ropes of priceless pearls; she inhales deeply the heady scent of garlands of flowers; she listens, entranced, to the tinkle of tiny finger cymbals; she drinks from a golden goblet and reels delightedly from the wine; her hands caress the contours and softnesses of her own body. For her dances of the five senses, the nearly nude goddess has been arrayed by her priests in a great circular golden skirt that swirls gently as she moves. But now she gives herself up to a total surrender to physical joys. This is the Delirium of the Senses dance, and she whirls, a golden flame, until she is spent and falls to the ground.

Slowly Radha arises and sheds the golden skirt, the symbol of worldly possessions. This is her renunciation of a life dedicated to physical pleasures. She returns to her dais and assumes the position of a statue of bronze. The goddess has danced her sermon, the priests have learned that they too must reject such pleasures in order to find *nirvana,* pure peace, pure purpose, pure self.

Martha, too, experienced a revelation. She was transported. She knew she had to be a dancer, good or bad. Here before her was a new world of color, of fantastic images, of beings caught up in ritual. This was indeed the very ritual she had sought and had partially found in the "music and costumes" of the Catholic mass that Lizzie had shown her. And here, too, was the exploration, below the surface of ceremony, of the very nature of human beings with their desires, frailties, and passions that she had found not in picture books and portraits but only in words. Now it had all come together in the magical theater of Ruth St. Denis.

The St. Denis dance was not only a revelation to Martha; it had been, for the barely five years since its invention, a revelation to audiences both in America and in Europe. To Europeans, this way of dance seemed new and daring simply because it was totally different from classical ballet, the "art" dance they were familiar with. And, of course, it had no resemblance to the tap or clog or social dancing Americans of the time knew.

Ballet, which had started out as a royal court spectacle in the palaces of dukes and kings three hundred years before, was much more of an "outer" dance than the "inner" dance impulses that St. Denis had conceived. In ballet there are five basic positions of the feet, and no matter where the dancers moved, they started from one of these positions and ended in one of them. There were comparable positions of the arms.

The body itself was customarily held erect, very elegantly, as one would expect of a dance devised by courtiers. For the most part, ballet is concerned with "a geometrical arrangement of numerous people dancing together under a diverse harmony of many instruments," as an early ballet master described it in 1581.

St. Denis was not interested in geometry. She was dealing in dance with God and guts. She used her arms and legs, of course, but not in movements set down by a method. The spur to action came from deep within, viscerally, emotionally. And although ballet danced about gods, the mythical gods of Greek and Roman legend, St. Denis, an American girl from a New Jersey farm, was determined to dance about a present God. This she did, first in the East Indian dances that Martha saw and years later in dances created for churches and synagogues.

Martha understood her purpose immediately; most other Americans did not. Dancing was supposed to be merely pretty, wasn't it? No one even dreamed of it as an equal to the arts of music, painting, literature. No one, that is, except Ruth St. Denis from Newark and her equally great contemporary from San Francisco, Isadora Duncan, who also fought to restore to modern dance its ancient dignity and spiritual force, through a rediscovery of the dance ideals of ancient Greece, its philosophy of human dignity and reverence for a free, unadorned body.

American newspaper reporters—there were no dance critics then—were at a loss to describe Ruth St. Denis. They described her as a beautiful woman, they commented delightedly on the fact that she wore fewer clothes (often a bare midriff and always, shocking to

say, bare feet!) than other performers. Then they began
to stumble all over themselves in confusion by saying
that although she might look physically desirable, she
was strangely spiritual. The reporters didn't know what
to make of it.

Martha Graham did. She wanted to be just like
Ruth St. Denis.

She told Dr. Graham of her intention. He would
have none of it. Martha was to finish school before
indulging herself in any such whims. And *no* dancing
lessons on the side! Dr. Graham, who had moved
permanently to California from Allegheny in 1912, was
there to see that he was obeyed. So Martha settled down
to finish her terms at Santa Barbara High School.

She gave up sports because she feared injury to her
legs, legs now dedicated to dancing. But she did
everything else expected of a high school girl. Her
favorite subject, naturally, was literature, and her high
school principal, Jane Carol Byrd, whom she always
referred to with admiration and deep affection, urged
her not only to explore the wealth of libraries but to
write herself.

In addition to literature and writing, Martha
excelled in both Spanish and German (she had two
years in each) and in Latin, which she studied for four
years. In fact, her performance as Dido in the school
play was all in Latin. She also earned top marks in
geometry.

After her high school graduation in 1913, Dr.
Graham was understanding enough to permit his oldest
daughter to enroll in an arts-oriented junior college, the
Cumnock School in Los Angeles. Here she would have
an opportunity to learn acting, to write not only stories

Martha at the time of her high school graduation.

but plays and, best of all, to have her first dance lessons. She had three lessons a week in dance "expression," a sort of free rhythmic kind of movement, often called "esthetic" or "interpretive" dancing. She was not alone among the students in her idolizing of St. Denis, and the chance to be near her idol came sooner than she expected. In 1915 Ruth St. Denis, with her young husband of one year, Ted Shawn (just two years older than Martha), opened a dance school in Los Angeles. Martha was not permitted to enroll, but the school was there, waiting for the day she would graduate from Cumnock.

Before she could make this fateful move, tragedy struck the Graham family. In 1914 Dr. Graham died. He and his daughter had crossed wills on many occasions, and his long absences from home, until two years before he died, had made his influence less steady than that of other fathers. Still, Martha was close to him, taking strength from his strength and understanding of people from his profound knowledge of human behavior. His loss was deeply felt.

Dr. Graham was not a rich man. He left little in cash, but he did leave California real estate in which he had invested rather heavily. But Mrs. Graham never for a moment questioned the continuation of her daughters' education. All three were to continue at all costs. Property was sold piece by piece over the years until there was almost nothing left. Martha was able to complete her studies and graduated from Cumnock in the late spring of 1916, shortly after her twenty-second birthday.

Immediately, she took the giant step and enrolled for the summer course at Denishawn, the Ruth St.

Denis and Ted Shawn School of Dancing in Los Angeles. It was an unusual dancing school. Some ballet was taught, just enough to train the body in a discipline that had evolved during three hundred years. But basically it was a school of total dance, for Ted Shawn believed in a dance that encompassed every way that humankind had moved rhythmically to express itself in any era, in any country, in any situation. Thus, at Denishawn, she joined students in classes in various forms of Oriental dance, Spanish dance, primitive dance, and anything else that came to the attention of the founders. The creed of Denishawn was a quotation from an essay, "The Dance of Life," written by one of the great psychologists of the era, Havelock Ellis. He had said, "If we are indifferent to the art of dancing, we have failed to understand not merely the supreme manifestation of physical life, but also the supreme symbol of spiritual life."

Martha agreed wholeheartedly with the credo, with the courses, with the school, with her teachers, and, of course, with her long-anticipated nearness to the goddess, Ruth St. Denis. There was only one hitch: St. Denis did not care for the new Denishawn student. In fact, she was, at first, so indifferent to her that she said to her husband, "You take her in your classes, Teddy dear, I don't know what to do with her."

Apprentice Years

Ted Shawn and Martha Graham started off with one bond in common: an adoration of St. Denis. Ted, a divinity student at the University of Denver, had first seen Ruth St. Denis dance in what was very probably the identical program that Martha was to see a few weeks later. All he needed was *The Incense* and, as he later put it, "I danced right out of the church and into the theater." Only in his wildest dreams did he think that he might someday have a lesson from her. But her inspiration led him to study ballet, read voluminously (as did Martha), study seconds of exotic dance fragments in movie travelogues, and finally found a little touring dance company.

His group made its way to New York in 1913. In 1914, when St. Denis put out a call for a male dancer to join her company, primarily to do popular ballroom dances with one of her girls, Ted Shawn applied for the job. She hired him almost on sight, soon promoted him to be her partner (although she refused to give him costar billing until close to the end of their joint career), and married him a few months after they met.

St. Denis never wanted a school. She wanted only to create dances and to perform. Shawn, an educator by instinct, wanted to teach his and St. Denis's new concept of total dance to others, to train a special group of dancers for a company, to make their work a household word. Reluctantly, St. Denis agreed, and Denishawn was born.

When Martha enrolled, the school was housed in a mansion of Spanish-style architecture. Although situated in the heart of Los Angeles, it was almost rural in atmosphere, for it was atop a hill and surrounded by groves of eucalyptus trees. There was a swimming pool, and the big outdoor studio was protected from inclement weather by canopies. Peacocks roamed the grounds. It was all very exotic, but Shawn saw to it that the students worked long and hard.

Martha was only a student, and a novice at that, but there was promise of performing opportunities almost instantly open to a talented newcomer, a quick learner. For Denishawn, even early in its life, was a big producing agency, a result mainly of Shawn's speed at choreography, his administrative skill, and his great organizing ability. Denishawn was not only a school but also a concert group and a source of separate vaudeville units, ensembles for dance, spectacle scenes in silent movies, and, enlarged by its students, available for pageants. Not long after her enrollment at Denishawn, Martha made her professional debut as a dancer in *A Dance Pageant of Egypt, Greece and India* at the Greek Theater in Berkeley, California. It was the first time that this still famous theater permitted a program of dancing under its prestigious banner. Martha had a minor place in the vast pageant, but there is a photo of her in Egyptian dress, her first theatrical portrait.

Shawn had coached her for her role. She had become his pupil for reasons that were not simply a St. Denis whim, although the great lady's likes and dislikes were observed without argument. Martha was small, intense, a woman with a dark, dour expression. St. Denis, a lyrical dancer, saw immediately that Martha did not move with that sweeping, flowing quality for which she herself was famous. "Miss Ruth," as she was called by all her students and dancers, felt that Shawn's sharper, stronger, more primitive style of movement would be better suited to the young pupil. But Martha was, of course, exposed to all kinds of dance. Her wide, big eyes silently took in everything. Her fellow students regarded her with interest and thought that when she moved there was a sense of abandon about her. She was, in their estimation, rather like a gypsy.

She learned dance gestures, steps, exercises as quickly as she had learned the contents of books. Her concentration awed her fellows, delighted Shawn, and even earned the somewhat grudging admiration of St. Denis who, toward the end of Martha's first year, occasionally used her to demonstrate movements for her in class. Neither Shawn nor St. Denis felt that she was ready to learn repertory, to master solo dances, but they

Her professional debut, as Priestess of Isis in a Denishawn pageant.

felt that what she had learned of basic exercises, she knew thoroughly. So they entrusted her with classes for the littlest pupils, some only three or four years old.

Martha led the children in running, skipping, and jumping patterns. Sometimes they were told to imitate animals. Most turned themselves into bunnies, frogs, deer, kittens, but one strange little girl, as strange as Martha, came up with an animal study that Martha couldn't recognize. "What are you supposed to be?" she asked. "A bird," replied the child. "But you don't look as if you are flying," said the teacher. The terse reply was, "I'm not. I'm a bird eating a worm."

Because she had shouldered her teaching responsibilities to the satisfaction of St. Denis and Shawn, Martha was permitted to sit unobtrusively in a corner and watch the more advanced girls learn Denishawn solos. She wasn't considered good enough to perform but looking at them would be all right.

At one such session, Martha was actually seeing a rehearsal of what was planned as a very special benefit performance given by the advanced pupils—almost professionals—of Denishawn. Shawn was teaching a solo called *Serenata Morisca*, a sensual, Moorish gypsy dance. He went over it four times as he rehearsed it with the girls. He glanced at Martha: "It's too bad Martha doesn't know this dance. She would look just right in it." Martha blurted, "But I do know it, Mr. Shawn." "Impossible," he answered, "you've only just seen it and never danced it." "But I know it! I know it!" she cried out. Shawn scowled. "Let me see."

Martha came out of the corner and danced. When she had finished, Shawn looked at her silently, intently. "Was it that bad, Mr. Shawn?" The answer was, "No.

A tango with Ted Shawn.

It was thoroughly professional in every way. You'll do it!"

From that time on *Serenata Morisca* swiftly became a Graham trademark. She danced it everywhere with Denishawn. It was her first solo. It transformed her from a student—to a professional. It made her a soloist in Denishawn, the greatest dance company in America.

Some years later *Serenata Morisca* would serve as the number that made her a dancing star in a Broadway show, a step in her climb to the rank of superstar in the wide world of dance. But it had all started in a comfortable studio with peacocks wandering about as Ted Shawn said, "Thoroughly professional!" predicting a great career for his strange pupil.

Martha fell heir to all sorts of jobs. In 1917, after the United States had entered World War I, Shawn enlisted in the Army. He was stationed at an officers' training school not far from Los Angeles and was able to get to the studio on weekends to teach. Martha studied with him, but she also continued to do some teaching for Denishawn. St. Denis was off on tour, either selling Liberty Bonds or performing or both. Her special protégée, Doris Humphrey, usually toured with her, and Martha, with not much experience, shouldered many of the responsibilities of the Denishawn School.

When the war ended late in 1918, Shawn was discharged. His wife had necessarily had her managers make bookings beyond that time for her and her group, not knowing how long the war would last. When Shawn returned he reestablished the school under his own name and made Martha his principal teacher. He joined St. Denis on many occasions for special appearances, but their professional careers were not to be reunited until 1921.

Vaudeville acts, as well as concert appearances, kept Shawn busy. He was especially adept at creating "art" dances for vaudeville in the days when movie houses, large or small, had at least five acts of vaudeville on every bill. One of Shawn's most popular vaudeville ballets was the lush fairy tale *Julnar of the Sea*, a headline act that toured constantly and successfully from 1919 through 1921. In 1920 he came up with another smash, *Xochitl*, an Aztec ballet, which starred Martha Graham.

Shawn did not create the work and then choose the dancer. *Xochitl* was made, almost tailor-made, for the uniqueness of Graham. Martha did not have the serene face of a St. Denis nor the full-blown pinkness of an Isadora Duncan. Her face, with its high cheekbones, made Shawn think of the Indians who built their civilizations in the Americas before Columbus and the first white men came. Besides, Martha was fierce in temperament and almost explosive in her energies. Shawn commissioned an original score, based on Mexican Indian themes, by the composer Homer Grunn and an elaborate setting and costumes by Francisco Cornajo, who had also supplied the story.

The story was about an Aztec (or more accurately, Toltec, the pre-Aztec civilization that the Aztecs absorbed) maiden, Xochitl, possessed of such beauty and fire that the Emperor falls in love with her and tries to take her for himself. She repels his advances at the risk of her life, but wins her fight to protect her virtue. Years later, Denishawn dancers (and Shawn himself) recalled that Martha was a terrifying figure of wildness and fury as the assaulted maiden.

Martha's first partner in the vaudeville company was handsome Robert Gorham, a Denishawn dancer. When Gorham was taken ill, a Denishawn newcomer,

With Robert Gorham, in *Xochitl*.

Charles Weidman, was sent in by Shawn as a replace-
ment. Martha was in a rage. She bared her teeth but to
no avail. Charles did not know the role, he was scrawny
and not, she felt, a proper foil. Weidman not only
became her dear friend but subsequently one of the
great pioneering leaders of that American modern
dance which, in the late 1920s, was to burst out of
Denishawn.

Xochitl not only played vaudeville, it also found its
way into the repertory of the Denishawn Dancers.
Shawn himself assumed the role of the Emperor (one of
his most effective characterizations), and he and Martha proceeded to give performances of shattering impact
for the audience and for each other. Shawn often
recalled during his long lifetime (he was past eighty
when he died) that Martha was ferocious in the dance
showing her efforts to preserve her virginity. "Sometimes my face would be bleeding when I came offstage.
Once she punched me so hard that there was a hole
under my lip right through to my teeth." Martha, at
eighty, smiled at me, baring her teeth prettily, and said,
"He was pretty rough too. Once he dropped me on my
head."

Xochitl was so successful that Martha danced in it
from coast to coast for two triumphant years as the
greatest junior star that Denishawn had produced. With
the concert group, she also danced *Serenata Morisca*,
Malagueña (a popular duet with Shawn), and a vast
array of Spanish, Javanese, Arabian, East Indian,
American Indian, Burmese, and other dances.

When the Denishawn Dancers went to London, St.
Denis suddenly decided that *Xochitl* was far too big a
plum for Martha, and although the role didn't suit her,

she took it away from Martha, after raging tantrums
with Shawn, and performed it herself. Shawn remembered that his wife, utterly feminine and yielding (at
least onstage), never put up much of a fight for her
virtue. "Sometimes," he said, "Ruth would put up no
battle at all in the seduction scene, but fairly swoon in
my arms and murmur, 'Darling, you're hurting me.'
And the ballet nearly had a different ending!" Martha
was hurt and upset, but it in no way undermined her
devotion to Miss Ruth.

Martha and Shawn, whom she was getting to like
less and less, had a brief period of closeness in the
"misery loves company" sense. St. Denis, in London,
was being exceptionally difficult, and Martha was
temporarily separated from her first real love, Louis
Horst, Denishawn's musical director. She had met
Horst long before London and the two had fallen in
love. Horst was married, but his wife, Betty, ran a
dancing school and did not usually go on tour. However, Betty did go to London, thus making it impossible
for Louis and Martha to maintain the pitch of their
romance. Shawn and Graham found themselves dining
together, going to museums together, and even, with an
appropriate sense of sad drama, walking together in the
rain.

But Martha, back home, was becoming restless.
Her always quick temper flared more often. Instead of
being in awe of Ted Shawn as she had been when a
student, she now began to question him both as an artist
and as an employer. She was no longer eager to perform
in dances rooted in foreign cultures, no matter how
exotic, but neither was she quite certain what she
wanted to do. She fumed but she stayed on. Having

danced many numbers staged by someone else, she now developed the urge to make dances for herself. She had not heard of the word "choreography"—it is doubtful that even St. Denis herself, highly literate as she was, was familiar with the term in the early '20s—she simply wanted to "make" dances.

Miss Ruth she truly loved, but she found Shawn increasingly arbitrary, with orders such as "You'll do this," "You'll dance that," "I have assigned you a job giving exercises to overweight women." Her temper grew. Once, when doing vaudeville, she insisted on including *Serenata Morisca* on the bill. She was told she couldn't; a telephone call was put through to Shawn who added a firm "No!" to her demands; she ripped the phone off the wall backstage and smashed it on the floor.

Another time, in New York, when Shawn told her that between engagements she would teach an exercise class for salesgirls, she stood up at the table in the restaurant where they were lunching and pulled the tablecloth—plates, silver, food, and all—off and onto the floor. She stormed out and got into a taxi. Shawn, with a temper to equal hers, followed and slammed the door of the cab so hard that panes of glass fell out into the street. Only when Miss Ruth took on a young lover in London and Martha temporarily lost her Louis to Betty, did Martha and Ted bury their animosities to share sorrow together.

Their basic dislike lasted all their lives. When they met, in later years, they embraced and exchanged platitudes, but privately the distaste continued. Once, in an interview, Martha omitted the Shawn name while talking of major dancers. She said, "Well, if you're

talking about artists, his name would hardly come up."
Shawn was no kinder, even in what should have been
his mellow years. He would condemn her for saying to
the press in later years that she was a pupil of St.
Denis's and not of Shawn's. The old man's eyes would
flash, "I trained her. Ruth didn't and wouldn't. There'd
be no Martha Graham without me." Two minutes
later, he would criticize her dancing and denounce her
choreography. Once, to me, he screamed, "She's anti-
Christ!" When I asked him which viewpoint he wanted
to espouse—that he couldn't have it both ways unless he
meant she was a dreadful, anti-Christ dancer and he
was responsible—he burst into tears. There was no love
lost there.

Martha was looking for a way out. At one point,
between tours, Shawn had recommended Martha to a
producer of musical revues, John Murray Anderson.
She auditioned, but she was so small and seemingly shy
and not at all pretty that Anderson dismissed her and
gave Shawn hell for having wasted his time. He had not
seen her, at that time, in things like *Xochitl.* Later he saw
her in *Serenata Morisca*, and, not recognizing her, asked
Shawn to release her. But Shawn needed her at that
time and refused.

When Martha finally left Denishawn, she went to
Anderson and asked for a job. He looked at her and
said, "No." She reminded him about *Serenata Morisca*
and said rather shyly, "I'm the girl you liked." He
gasped his disbelief, but he hired her. With makeup on
and gorgeous costumes and settings, she was transformed. Anderson was ecstatic. So was the public.
Martha Graham remained the dance star of the
Greenwich Village Follies for two years, from 1923 to 1925.

Star of the *Greenwich Village Follies.*   NICKOLAS MURAY

Like most revues of the time, the *Follies* went from one edition to another. This meant that although the show itself continued to run indefinitely, the artists changed acts from time to time. New material was added, and for skits based on current affairs updating was in order. Customers would return to see new acts in a show they already liked. Martha did the same. At last she had a chance to make up her own dances, but Anderson would never let her stray far from the exotic, mysterious, sensual creature of *Serenata Morisca.* For him, she always had to be glamorous, and he insisted that in her dances she use fanciful costumes, colorful scarves, scenery, and props that would make her seem like some rare importation from a foreign land—Spain, India, or even a Parisian cellar club. So she danced not only the old *Serenata Morisca* but also *The Garden of Kama* from Indian sources, a Spanish potpourri, and anything that might be classified in the vaudeville jargon of the day as "an art spot" or "a class act."

Martha was now a Broadway star, but she lived an austere, almost Puritan life, a life dedicated to dance and to her own career. She had many admirers, but she didn't want them and she didn't need them. Earlier, when she was in Denishawn vaudeville, she had said to a then obscure manager, Samuel Rothafel (he became the legendary "Roxy," first boss of the Radio City Music Hall, with a mammoth movie palace on Broadway named after him), "I'm going to the top. Nothing is going to stop me. And I shall do it alone."

She didn't need rich and influential men. But she did need guidance from those she trusted. Louis Horst was one. But Martha was and always would be a "loner." She had to get to wherever she was going by herself, no matter how tortuous the routes or tortured the heart. The path she took is recorded in the very title of one of her greatest dances, *Errand into the Maze*, created many years later.

While performing in vaudeville and the *Follies* for money and experience, she was well aware of the fact that she was, or could be, an artist. The word "artist" held no fancy meaning for her. It didn't necessarily mean a person who was famous, glamorous, and sought-after—those were by-products. It meant what it would always mean to her: "Artist means 'worker' to me. It is not a very good word, but it is still the best word to describe someone who works for what he believes in."

She believed in it so thoroughly that in 1925, despite her fans, friends, and a very good salary, she said to herself, "Enough of this. I'm going on to more important things." She left the *Follies*, modest fame, and security. As far as Broadway was concerned, she disappeared from view. She exchanged the stage for a school. She had, at thirty, much more to learn. Curiously, though, she was her own teacher.

Revolt

Martha's move took her to Rochester, New York, where she was appointed codirector, with Esther Gustafson, of a newly established dance department at the Eastman School of Music. The school had been founded by George Eastman, who had invented in 1888 a device for taking snapshot photographs and called it Kodak. Eastman was also a philanthropist and a lover of music. For his opera department, he had engaged the gifted Russian-born director Rouben Mamoulian. Later Mamoulian's brilliance would be responsible for such successes as *A Farewell to Arms* (the movie), *Porgy* (the play), *Porgy and Bess* (the opera), and *Queen Christina* (the movie with Garbo). Mamoulian, in turn, engaged

Martha for Eastman because of his admiration for her as a dancer and a Broadway performer.

Miss Gustafson was, according to Martha, of the Isadora Duncan school of free, expressive dance, while Martha herself was a product of the highly theatrical Denishawn, which had always put its free movements into elaborate theater form.

Martha arrived at Eastman with the zeal of a biblical prophet, assured that away from the controls and confining range of Broadway she could be exactly the kind of artist she pleased. She was proud, determined, very touchy (her temper grew with her skills), and determined to do exactly what she wanted. Heaven help whoever got in her way.

Her intensive stage and classroom experience at Denishawn and her mastery of show business had prepared her physically for her Eastman duties. She had a highly trained body. Now she had to find the "being" that was Martha Graham. As she began her experiments, free for the first time of outside demands and pressures, the echo of her father's words came back to her: "The body does not lie. . . ."

Thus, while teaching others at Eastman, she was also teaching herself. Louis Horst left Denishawn the year that Martha went to Eastman, but even though he traveled to Vienna to study modern music, the composer and the dancer began to grow closer than ever before. Now both were at last free of the theater world of Denishawn and eager to explore new paths. Louis was disenchanted with the accomplishments of modern music in Central Europe, but he had been impressed with modern dance in Germany. It was a new form of theatrical dancing introduced by Rudolf von Laban

Graham (center) with two of her Eastman students,
Evelyn Sabin (left) and Betty MacDonald (right).

WITZEL

and his brilliant pupil, Mary Wigman. They too had broken away from the conventions of classical ballet, moving even further along the pathway toward a liberated dance than Duncan and St. Denis.

Accepted, respected, and immensely influential elsewhere in Europe long before they were fully understood in their homeland, von Laban and Wigman had changed the face of dance in Europe. The world of ballet seemed inadequate to them to express the devastation and desperation of postwar Europe. Ballet's fairies and elves, sleeping beauties and prince charmings seemed incongruous. So did much of the light and frothy music usually written for ballet. Even the music of the great composers that Isadora Duncan had commandeered for her art of dance seemed too noble. Wigman built a movement technique for dance on the principles of tension (tightening the muscles) and relaxation (expelling all energy), and her dance themes culminated in a terrifying work of great power, *Totenmal*, monument to the dead. It wasn't pretty. Neither was her music. She turned to drums and gongs—the sonorities and hammering insistencies of percussion. Her themes were percussive, her dances percussive, her music percussive, the effect she wanted to make, percussive.

News of Wigman drifted to America long before she herself arrived with her company in 1930.

Ted Shawn used to say that Louis Horst, returned from Europe, led Martha into a new and "ugly" dance and that he had seen Martha and Louis studying pictures of Wigman and discussing them avidly. But this he later revised, when he decided to claim Martha as his product. Then he said that her use of tension came from his training of her in primitive dances and that his own special classes in expressive movement had guided her.

The truth of it is that modern dance developed independently, but almost simultaneously, in America and in Europe. The climate was right for a rebellion against a dance that was too decorative for postwar tastes. Change was essential for those artists who wanted to speak for their times, most of all for one innovator who wanted dancing bodies "to tell the truth."

At Eastman, Martha could involve others in her experiments. She was no longer alone. From her students, she selected three girls—Evelyn Sabin, Betty MacDonald, Thelma Biracree—to become her first dance group.

She showed Louis the first dances she had composed. "Horrid little things," he said. She cried and yelled and disagreed. But she listened to him—in between fights and tantrums. Louis saw more in her than she had yet found in herself. He recognized genius in her, and it was up to him as musician, composer, teacher, friend, and confidant, as well as lover, to help her to release what she later called "divine discontent" in a torrent of creative energy.

On April 18, 1926, she emerged from her self-imposed obscurity to give her first independent concert in New York City at the Forty-eighth Street Theater. Her three Eastman workshop girls constituted her company. There were no startling changes in this debut program. Martha had choreographed the entire program, and Louis, her accompanist, had been her adviser, yet the influence of Denishawn was still far more than an echo. The titles of some of her first dances reveal this: *Three Gopi Maidens, Maid with the Flaxen Hair, The Moth, Florentine Madonna, Clair de Lune.* Newspaper reporters found her and her dances decorative and pretty. No, there was nothing disturbing here.

But something was happening behind the scenes. Martha was preparing for her second recital and the lid was about to blow off. The "graceful" and "gentle" girl who made "pretty pictures" would, within a matter of months, be described as "ugly" and "stark." In 1926 she was described as "lacking power." In 1927 she jolted her audience in a new solo called *Revolt.* Perhaps this dance contained her own angry rebellion against Denishawn, but more important, it revealed her concern with man's injustice to man. She had discovered that she did indeed possess the power to speak—and eloquently—through movement, of her deepest feelings.

In 1927, and in the New York appearances of the following years, the public (except for a new cult of Graham followers) and the press were outraged by such successors to *Revolt* as *Heretic, Vision of the Apocalypse, Immigrant, Four Insincerities.* The exotic woman was gone. She was not entertaining the public—she was disturbing them. And that was her intention.

What had she been doing in her classes and workshops at Eastman? She had, of course, no interest whatsoever in classical ballet other than as an established system, suitable to those who liked it, of body training. Martha was running against the tide. In the 1920s thousands of little girls from one end of the country to the other dreamed of becoming ballerinas. Their idol was the Russian star, Anna Pavlova, and the dance they adored was *The Dying Swan.* It was sad and it was beautiful, as Pavlova's arms fluttered like wings and

Anna Pavlova.

her feet, in toe shoes, skimmed the stage as if she were floating on water.

Martha, while respecting Pavlova as a remarkable artist, nevertheless felt that the Russian was confined by an antiquated dance system and insisted that she did not want to imitate a dying bird or, for that matter, a living one. If there was any dying to be done it would be the only kind of dying pertinent to her. It would be a human death. And it wouldn't be pretty. It would be harsh and tragic and perhaps even ugly. And it might not be a literal death—it could be the death of the spirit or of hope, a far more awful death than a physical one.

In the 1920s and '30s audiences still expected dance to be pretty, exotic, and filled with perilous acrobatic tricks. If you wanted something serious, you went to a play, read a book, or attended the symphony. You might even journey to Italy to look at "The Last Supper" or the "Pièta." You went to see dance to be stirred by feats of skill or to be transported into a world of fairies, pixies, nixes, dryads, and maybe uncomplicated young romance.

True, Ruth St. Denis and Isadora Duncan had upset the idea that dancing was fluff and froth. St. Denis had wanted to dance about God, but the gods she picked were foreign and mysterious and she herself was so beautiful that one really didn't have to bother oneself with what she was dancing about—just looking was enough. When she was an old lady, St. Denis once said to me, "I'm afraid many people in my audiences never saw beyond the trappings. If I had it to do over again, I'd begin with the Christian God. But then, I suppose, no one would have come to see me."

Isadora sometimes danced to symphonies, and her

themes were rooted in the potential nobility of man, but her unorthodox life, her many lovers, and her illegitimate children drew audiences to her as a "personality." Besides, however tragic and monumental her own solos, her girls, including her six adopted daughters, the Isadorables, danced sweetly and prettily in their Greek tunics.

But Martha? She had never been interested in paintings or drawings of people. She had preferred her portraits written in words in books. Here at Eastman she was beginning to think in terms of portraits in movement, biographies of human beings, which would show not how they looked but how they felt. Instead of creating plays about people with words, she wanted such characters to speak for themselves through *movement*. She was discovering that movement could be as eloquent as words. Somewhere, perhaps from Shawn, she had heard an old, old saying. A poet, a troubador, a wandering minstrel in medieval France had said, "That which *cannot* be spoken can be sung; that which *cannot* be sung can be danced!" She believed that an eloquence more profound than either words or music or both combined resided in dance.

As for music itself, she had her own ideas about its relationship to dance. She did not want to dance *to* music; she wanted to dance *with* it. In her first experiments she looked about for music already composed that would be suitable to her dance themes, music that would support through rhythm, timbre, pulse, and character her feelings and the passions of those secret characters she was to portray. Soon, she had Louis composing for her, writing music that gave voice to her ideas.

Horst, though an explorer and experimenter like Martha herself, was a scholar solidly grounded in traditional music. For his disciplines, he went to those preclassic dance forms—pavane, galliard, saraband, gigue, bourrée—which not only served as the musical units of ballet composition in the seventeenth and eighteenth centuries but which also formed the basis of the musical suite (carried to perfection by Johann Sebastian Bach) and its descendants in the sonata and the symphony. His music for Martha's *Primitive Mysteries* and *Frontier* sounded new and avant-garde, but the structures were solid and proven.

At Eastman, Martha's key investigation was focused on her body, its potentialities and its limitations. She knew well that ballet dancers were almost always erect, except perhaps in pantomime scenes, and that the physical excitement of their actions was based on defiance of gravity. Isadora, like St. Denis, had used the gravitational pull for dramatic and emotional effect. Ballet dancers moved backwards, forwards, and sideways, varied by diagonals. Martha felt that the dancer should be aware of more than the usual north, south, east, and west directions. She added up and down, as does the American Indian, to the key directions of the world. Frequently her dance movements took her down to the floor. "The floor *is* a direction," she said. When dancing about moments of despair, she did not simply bow her head downward, she permitted her entire body to sink downward. "When you are very upset," she would say, "you have a sinking feeling inside you. So as a dancer I showed on the *outside* what was happening on the *inside*—my whole body sank or fell to the floor."

She also came to believe that the back was the most

important part of the body. "It is magic," she would say. I remember watching her teach a class of college students, none of them professional dancers. They were sitting on the floor and doing an elaborate sequence of stretching exercises that Martha had devised over the years. Wearing a brocaded robe and dark glasses, she walked among them, making a correction here, giving a nod of approval there. She stopped by one sweating youth who was straining rather than strengthening his body. "My child, my child," she said. "Remember the divinity of your spine. It is your own tree of life. Everything branches out from it." Whether he understood her analogy is doubtful, but unquestionably he responded to the touch of an instructive hand.

In 1926 Martha knew but would not admit that the great ballet dancers, perhaps by instinct, used more than their brilliant legs and feet and lovely arms when dancing. Their backs were strong and their torsos, though not used with the gut power of the modern dancer, did move with the breath and pulse of life. In her own classes at Eastman and in the years that followed she invented exercises that would make her students conscious of the floor, aware of the power of the back, certain that the most intense feelings were revealed not simply in the gestures of hands but in powerful contractions, releases, stretchings, pullings, and spasms of the muscles of the torso.

Martha, along with other rebel dancers of the time, began to realize that their art could speak for the times in which they lived. Dancing, they were convinced, should not only concern itself with the fairy tales of ballet, the exotic productions of Denishawn, the joyous rhythms of the tap dancer, and the dancing of boys and

Students in a Graham class are made aware of the floor,
and of the power of the spine.

girls moving about a ballroom floor or a school gymna-
sium to the hit tunes of the day. Dancing should also
deal with such serious matters as poverty, racial bias,
neuroses, and even war. Some of these dances would not
be entertaining—any more than Shakespeare's *Hamlet*
or Ibsen's *Ghosts*, about the syphilitic destruction of a
mind, are. They would be disturbing to the mind and to
the guts. They would demand that audiences feel
deeply and think deeply.

Some kind of tag had to be given to this new dance
that was not ballet. "Esthetic" and "interpretive,"
barely suitable for the free dance forms generated by
Duncan and St. Denis, could hardly be used to describe
Martha's *Revolt* or *Heretic*. So the term "modern dance"
came into usage. It was intended as a stopgap descrip-
tion. The "moderns" never liked it, but they were stuck
with it. Martha avoided it almost entirely, and if she felt
it necessary to qualify her dance in some way, she
always used the word "contemporary."

In her crusade for a new dance Martha at first
walked alone on this side of the Atlantic. But five years
after her departure from Denishawn two of her former
colleagues and costars, Doris Humphrey and Charles
Weidman, also sought a way to make dance into a
serious commentator on a turbulent age. Tamiris, not
from Denishawn but with a background in a sort of
"interpretive" dance distantly related to Duncan and
with a touch of ballet, was the first to speak out in dance
about the appalling treatment of blacks in America,
although she herself was white. She had been simply
Helen Becker but took the name of an indomitable
Persian Queen, Tamiris, for the stage. Much later she
combined the two as Helen Tamiris. She called her

dance work *How Long Brethren*. It was one of the first
dances of social comment, as was Martha's *Revolt* and
her later protest against fascism in Spain in the solo
Deep Song.

These were difficult times for modern dance. They
were especially difficult for Martha, who had enjoyed a
certain amount of security at Denishawn, in the *Follies*,
and at Eastman, which she left soon after launching her
concert career. Behind her was the prettiness of dancing, a salable commodity. Many of the things she
wanted to dance about were spare, if not stark or
downright ugly. She dressed herself, after that first
recital, in severe costumes, often jerseys, so that the
unadorned body could be seen without scarves, veils,
jewels, trappings. Later she was to refer to the late 1920s
and early '30s as "the period of long woolens." She had
no desire to alienate an audience. Much later, in her
glamorous position as the sumptuously dressed grand
dame of the dance, she would smile and say, "I don't
know why any of them stuck with me, but they did. I
wanted people to like me, but I had to dance what I was
compelled to do and if the public hated me, well . . .
I'd rather have them hate me than be indifferent to
me."

If Martha was giving her audiences a rough time,
she was no less hard on herself. This was a time for
discipline as well as for discovery. "You have a beautiful
body just to begin with," she said to herself. "But that's
not enough. You must transform it through training.
Freedom is attained only through discipline. You must
train for ten years before you can become a dancer, a
good dancer. You may feel beautiful and gifted and
filled with all sorts of wonderful notions. But the stage is

not the place for a happy accident. You may think of
yourself as an angel and just beautifully ready to go
onstage without any preparation. If you do, you'll
probably fall on your face—and you'll deserve to!"

So Martha disciplined that beautiful instrument
remorselessly. She stretched every muscle to its utmost.
She worked on blood circulation and breathing, sinews
and tendons and tissues and even viscera. Yes, the
unseen viscera were worked on in a new kind of
movement principle she called "contraction and release." Everyone could see the outer shape of the body.
Martha was equally concerned with the inner structure
of the body.

While Germany's Mary Wigman had worked on
tension and relaxation and all the degrees of energy
lying between these two poles, Martha did not use
relaxation. She never relaxed. Contraction was like a
clenched fist; releasing it would be to return to a normal
state, not floppy in complete relaxation. She could do
the same with fingers, a shoulder, a foot, any place with
a muscle. If she contracted her entire torso as an
expectant mother might do to aid the delivery of a
baby, the contraction, if sufficiently forceful, could carry
her body from an upright position right down to the
floor. In Martha's mind such actions could be the very
stuff of dramatic dance, revealing the inside on the
outside.

She thought of a house. It has an inside as well as
an outside. What happens on the inside is what matters.
The same, she knew, was true of the body. Comparing
the dancer's body with architecture was not as odd as it
seemed. Martha had heard Ted Shawn say long before
at Denishawn that the two oldest arts in the history of

the world were dance and architecture. When primitive man lived in a cave for shelter, he found architecture waiting for him, supplied by nature. Only later did he himself begin to build, to design houses, palaces and temples, to make sculptures and paintings. Man, before he knew a language, could express himself in movement and his first art expression was to dance. From his dances, with the expulsion of breath, came words and words grew into sentences, poems, into songs, into drama. Martha, in her new dance experiments, was linking up the two oldest accomplishments of man— movement and structure.

The key combination, contraction and release, was all-important, not only to the new Graham training methods but also to the excitement of theater itself. The action that triggered, or generated, the contraction and release of muscles was breathing. "Miss Ruth" had used breathing, dramatizing it for effect, but the earlier pioneer had used breathing instinctively. Martha "organized" breathing for her stage purposes. Taking in the breath was a "release"; squeezing it out was a "contraction." Anyone, by exaggerating normal inhaling and exhaling, can experience the effect Martha wanted.

The Graham technique, then, was based on the concept of the body as a breathing instrument that could be seen. One did not simply "hear" the dancer breathe—preferably the breathing would be unheard, since sounds of breathing would suggest effort—but "see" the body breathe. "Not heave, but breathe," Martha said. By controlling the use of breath, she could govern the elements of drama onstage. Thus, when quiet, still moments came along in a dance, there would

be an aura of tension, of anticipation, because the body
was accustomed to regular breathing.

The breath, she knew (as did St. Denis, Duncan,
and her own contemporary, Doris Humphrey), had a
rhythm all its own. It was an emotional rhythm,
because a departure from the normal intake and
outflow of breath was the result either of effort or of
emotional experience. In this sense it differed from
metric rhythm, the applied-from-the-outside beats of a
march or a waltz or any musical form. Martha's
contractions and releases made for special body
rhythms that, although different from the outside
rhythms of music, could be interrelated to high dramatic effect.

Martha worked in phrases of action—dramatic,
comic, passionate, violent, tender—and, she later recalled, "I began to understand what we really meant by
that word 'phrase.' It meant 'breath-length.' If you're
angry your breath-lengths are short and your phrases
are staccato and short, but in something like the
'Liebestod' in *Tristan and Isolde* where the characters are
taking forever to die, you have long, long phrases. To
this day, when I'm choreographing, I still use the phrase
'breath-length' instead of the metric count."

To ballet dancers and followers such anatomical
exploration as Martha—and later Doris and Charles
and Tamiris—conducted seemed pretentious. Take
your ballet lesson, learn the five positions of the feet,
hold the body erect, kick, turn, jump, balance. Just
dance! Martha was equally contemptuous of ballet. She
did not realize it then, but she would one day state that
ballet was not to be ignored. "It would be a criminal
waste," she said many years later, "not to take advan-

tage of three hundred years of ballet development. My quarrel was never with ballet itself but that, as used in classical ballets, it did not say enough, especially when it came to intense drama, to passion. It was that very lack that sent me into the kind of work I do, so that I could get beyond the surface and to that inner world."

This "inner world" in dance was not to everyone's liking. An actress-friend of Miss Ruth's, attending an early Graham recital, went backstage and said, "Martha, how long do you expect to keep up this dreadful dancing?" And Martha replied, "As long as I have an audience." Even Martha's mother was far from enchanted with the new Graham. She did not see the first controversial programs, but when Martha and her company made their first California tour, where Mrs. Graham had remained following her second marriage to Homer Duffy, Mrs. Duffy, so the story goes, murmured to a friend, "I remember when Martha used to dance pretty things."

It wasn't that Martha didn't care about an audience. She did. She cared about them enough to chastise them into paying attention to what she had to say, through movement. She was giving them something they had never had before.

"You are a great public servant," she told her dancers. "You are fulfilling a person's dream of what a man and a woman *can* be or should *beware* of being. Sometimes you are doing something for them because they cannot do it for themselves, at least not in the same way. So you are a servant to the public and that is a great privilege and a great honor.

"I'm afraid I used to hit audiences over the head with a sledgehammer because I was so determined that

they see and feel what I was trying to do. Now I know
that you don't hit them as I first did or throw roses at
them as some entertainers do, but that you must draw
people to you, like a magnet. I'm not quite sure how
you become that magnet—perhaps by the intensity of
your own belief. I do know that a dancer must have two
things: a highly developed body technique and the
ability to draw people to you. The first can be taught;
the second cannot."

Martha was always that magnet. Martha was
always a star. Martha could draw people to her. She did
it as a child, she did it at Denishawn, she did it as the
star of her own company. For sixty years she was one of
the most powerful magnets on the American stage.
Retired from the stage as a dancer, she was still a
magnet, for all she needed to do was enter a room and
all eyes were upon her, riveted.

When she first came to New York with her
revolutionary dances she magnetized as well as repelled
people. Intellectually, as well as artistically, she won the
lasting admiration and friendship of Frances Steloff,
owner of one of New York's most prestigious bookshops,
the Gotham Book Mart. She fairly hypnotized, at her
first performances, a young educator who had studied
ballet and later free dance form and physical education.
Her name was Martha Hill. She was, for a while, a
Graham dancer, but later, combining her knowledge
and passion for dance with her schooling in traditional
physical education and an incredible organizing skill,
she became a pioneering power in advancing the cause
of dance in colleges and universities.

Before Martha Hill, dancing in school was almost
exclusively folk dancing for girls, with occasional splur-
ges into rhythmic gymnastics. Dr. Margaret H'Doubler

(not much older than Martha Hill, her student) had introduced dance, as a credit course, into the physical education program at the University of Wisconsin. It was modern dance, not folk. An entry for the "new" dance was made by way of the physical education door. It wasn't treated as an art (except in the minds of people like H'Doubler and Hill) but as an activity. You could, as a student, "take" basketball or dance, it didn't matter. This was not ideal, but it was a way to build modern dance at the right age level—with the young.

Martha Hill exercised such increasing influence that she was able, through her own energies, contacts, and such organizations as the American Association for Health, Physical Education and Recreation, to make dance a viable part of the curriculum in many college physical education departments. H'Doubler did the same for a band of colleges in the central part of the country. Hill literally took over the whole Atlantic seaboard and, eventually, through her own college pupils, exerted her influence at universities on the Pacific seaboard. The technique she espoused? Graham! And so too did her hundreds of pupils, all with respectable college degrees, which made them acceptable to institutions of higher learning. Once engaged as instructors, they could establish dance groups or classes within the framework of physical education programs. College girls were learning Graham technique, and when Martha and her company later made their tours, the enthusiastic nucleus of an otherwise hostile audience would be those college girls who knew the difference between a "contraction" and a "release."

Martha Hill's first campaign headquarters was New York University, where she was director of dance (starting 1931), then colleges in the strategic Middle and Far West, and, ultimately, little Bennington College in Vermont where modern dance, and Martha Graham, would make history in the 1930s.

Graham's magnetism with her students was pure sorcery. At the Robert Milton–John Murray Anderson School of Theatre where she began to teach after leaving Rochester, she found that young actors responded enthusiastically to her ability to give them expressive movement. One such student, a shy but determined New Englander, went on to become one of the greatest screen actresses of the century, Bette Davis. Miss Davis, in later years, described her feelings about Martha Graham simply and succinctly: "I worshipped her."

Martha's pupils in those decades were fanatical in their support of her. One of her later students, who became a star dancer in her company and a favored teacher of her technique, said to me not long ago, "Lots of people think she's a bitch, but they've got the consonant wrong—it's a 'w' not a 'b,' because she really is a witch. We're all under her spell."

Those who were not Graham pupils in the early years of modern dance were equally fanatical about their own teachers. The gossip and allegations in the 1930s were not to be believed. Anti-Grahamites would whisper, "Did you hear about so-and-so? Martha twisted her so hard that her spine broke through her skin!" Or, "Did you know that Martha's contractions are so terrible that she's had to have all her insides taken out. She doesn't have *anything* left inside her!"

Whatever Martha did or did not have in the 1920s and 1930s, she had genius. And it began its most abundant flowering when she was forty years old.

A New Frontier

Through teaching, Martha just about made ends meet. Louis made music for her and she sewed her own costumes, a habit she never gave up. She could decide at a dress rehearsal that certain costumes were wrong and she would rip them apart, sit on the floor, and remake them until they suited her. She also paid her dancers mainly through love, coaching, and, of course, witchcraft.

Modern dancers were not in the business for money. They were rarely paid. Ten dollars a performance was standard and ten or twelve performances a year wasn't a bad average. Rehearsal pay? Unheard of! There were no dancers' unions to fight for a living wage.

Graham dancers or Humphrey–Weidman dancers, all modern dancers worked as waitresses, clerks, delivery boys (though there were few males in dance then). It was arranged so that they worked by day and studied dance, rehearsed, and performed by night.

A talented teen-ager, invited to join the Humphrey-Weidman company and discovering that she'd earn about $100 a year, exclaimed, "But how do I live?" Charles Weidman countered, "Do you know how to operate an elevator?" The answer was "No." The response was "Then learn." Harriette Ann Gray did just that, survived, danced successfully, and eventually became the dance head of Stephens College in Missouri and director of a huge summer dance festival in the Rockies. (She can still run an elevator manually.)

Since Martha never liked the term "modern dance" and used it rarely, her school is called the Martha Graham School of Contemporary Dance. The school has, for some years, been housed in a lovely brick building, with a garden, in New York City. Two enormous studios provide space, airiness, and cheery light to students ranging in age from nine years into maturity. Admission, except for professional dancers, is by audition with Martha and her staff as judges.

The school's enrollment is approximately two hundred, and a faculty of ten (sometimes slightly more or slightly less) is responsible for six hundred class-hours per week in courses ranging from introductory (for those who have had no previous dance training whatever) through the beginners, intermediates, advanced, and professionals. All newcomers, no matter what their degree of dance proficiency, are required to start in the beginners class in order to become thoroughly familiar

with the fundamentals of the Graham system of training, which varies from that of other modern dance
teachers. (The basic technique of classical ballet is
universal, but modern dance techniques are the working methods of teachers with differing approaches.)
When Martha is not on tour with her company—she
travels with her troupe even though she no longer
dances—she teaches one class a day and at least one
class in each of the five levels each week.

In addition to the technique classes, the school
offers a teen-age workshop in Graham repertory and
choreography. This is always conducted by a highly
experienced professional dancer and choreographer,
someone such as Pearl Lang, who is Graham-trained, a
featured guest artist in the Graham company, and also
head of her own troupe as star and choreographer.

Some dance schools have separate classes, as well
as combined ones, for boys and girls. In classical ballet
there can be *pointe* (or toe shoe technique) classes for
girls, and classes for men, which stress leaps and air
turns and other muscular virtuosities. But all Graham
classes are mixed. All students are required to take a
minimum of two classes per week. The only exceptions
are professional dancers who, because of their own
performing, rehearsing, and touring schedules, may
take a class whenever they are free. This could be twice
a day, once a week, once a month, or whenever the
dancer's work schedule permits.

As the school expands, as it constantly does in
services offered, new courses are added. The newest are
courses in dance movement for actors, music training
for dancers, and related theatrical studies. Already the
school provides specially designed classes in modern

dance for ballet dancers who intend to remain in ballet but wish to extend their body capabilities beyond their own basic ballet technique and ballet classes for modern dancers who wish to experience the discipline of classical dancing.

The school, of course, feeds new talent into the Martha Graham Dance Company from time to time, although company members are also drawn from other sources (schools and companies in both America and in foreign lands).

In the first days of modern dance there was no such thing as a "season" or an engagement in any city, not even New York. This pertained to ballet also, for there were no ballet companies. The closest thing to a season would happen only in major cities and then but rarely, and the dance protagonists would be Ruth St. Denis and Ted Shawn and their Denishawn Dancers. Such was their popularity that they could play more than one performance in the same city. But they were alone in this accomplishment. Of course, if Anna Pavlova and her troupe appeared in vaudeville, the whole show, with other acts (comics, acrobats, musical seals, trained cockatoos, or whatever), would play a week or more. But not dance alone.

Dancers, for want of a better word, called their single appearances "recitals" or "concerts." Newspaper editors, not having any dance critics, looked at those terms and naturally assigned music critics to review. This was another burden to be borne by the growing dance in America, for music critics were rarely sympathetic. A drama critic would have been better. In the 1930s, when there were a handful of dance critics, Martha Graham used to say when she went on tour, "If I can't be reviewed by a dance critic, I would prefer a sportswriter over a music critic. Music critics listen to me dance and that's all wrong. The sportswriter might not understand my characters onstage, but he can see and appraise the only instrument the dancer has, a body, and he can see how well that body is disciplined, trained, perfected. He'd be starting from the right premise."

It was pressure from the Denishawners that launched dance criticism as a profession in the newspaper field. St. Denis and Shawn pointed out to publishers and editors that a minor musician would be given the courtesy of a review by a trained music critic whereas they, the great Denishawn company, could play record-breaking engagements at, say, Carnegie Hall in New York and receive barely a mention. In 1927 dance critics were appointed. First came Mary Watkins for the New York *Herald Tribune*, and a few weeks later, John Martin for *The New York Times*.

The irony was that Martin, with considerable experience in the little-theater and experimental theater movement, sought to prepare himself for his new post by talking with, observing, and getting to know the dancers residing in New York. These were the modern dancers, whose antipathy for ballet and near-contempt for the Denishawn from which they had sprung would influence the new critic. Martin's first review of Denishawn was devastating. Miss Ruth wept for days. Shawn raged for the next thirty years. When American ballet movements began, Martin dismissed them by saying that ballet was not and could not be an American dance expression. (He changed his mind some years later.) Watkins, fortunately, reviewed the moderns, the Denishawners, and ballet, each by their own standards.

Martha had left Denishawn with a clear-cut divorce. Doris and Charles had wanted to work out their reforms within the Denishawn institution. Doris was close to Miss Ruth and didn't want to hurt her. But Shawn was adamant in his control of Denishawn. He added modern dance to the curriculum by engaging the splendid Swedish dancer Ronny Johansson, but it was too late, although Ronny was respected and even loved by the American moderns. The fact that Shawn had refused his own dancers the right to engage in a new dance form of their own devising made the moderns resent both his arrogance and his lack of understanding. Many years later the moderns made peace with St. Denis, but with Shawn it was, at best, an armed truce.

The pioneering moderns weren't much kinder to each other. Martha would not permit her students to study anywhere else, and Doris and Charles were adamant about keeping their own dancers in near bondage. The adventuresome did sneak off to take classes with a rival teacher, but if caught, they were in danger of banishment. Martha was probably the worst offender. She demanded blind loyalty, and woebetide a Graham dancer who was discovered to have taken a ballet lesson or a Humphrey class.

On the top echelon, the former Denishawners were friendly enough. Martha would invite Charles and Doris to see a workshop, then call and say they shouldn't come, and finally worry that they wouldn't show up. Doris just put it down to "Martha's emotional insecurities." With male dancers rare, and none at all in the Graham group, Martha danced with Charles on several special occasions.

Martha, at this point, was anti-Denishawn, anti-romance, anti-curves, anti-establishment, anti-collaborations. Indeed, she was so curve-free in her angular movements that when Graham students first saw classical ballet with its rounded arms and flowing lines, they found it "distorted"!

In a lecture in collaboration with John Martin she snapped at a man in the audience who challenged her statements and beliefs: "Obviously, you don't know anything about movement!" He identified himself as Michel Fokine, one of ballet's great choreographers and himself an innovator with such works as *Petrouchka*, *Firebird*, *Les Sylphides*, *Scheherazade*, and *Prince Igor*. Umpired by Martin, Martha backed down a little when she realized to whom she was speaking. Later, when she was engaged to appear as the character The Chosen in a production of Stravinsky's ballet *Le Sacre du Printemps*, choreographed by Leonide Massine, the disagreements led to spectacular fights, which not even the great conductor Leopold Stokowski could quell. Finally it was performed, and by a miracle, without bloodshed.

Fokine, on his part, was as opinionated, as biased, as unreasonable as Graham. In my first job as dance critic for the Boston *Herald* in the 1930s I interviewed the great ballet master. I asked his opinion of modern dance as represented by the Graham technique.

He said to me, "Ugly girl makes ugly movements on stage while ugly mother tells ugly brother to make ugly sounds on drum. That is Graham's modern dance."

I asked him if he wasn't, however, sympathetic to an experimenter in dance, since he himself had rebelled against the ballet style he had been born into and had even been strongly influenced by Isadora Duncan.

He replied, "I liberated the dance. There is no place further to go."

There is nothing more conservative or reactionary than an aging rebel, I thought.

Though Martha was a loner, circumstances forced her, for financial reasons, out of her own orbit. After teaching at the Milton–Anderson school, she began decades of association with the Neighborhood Playhouse in New York. It was here that she was able to carry her dramatic theories beyond dance and into theater. An array of young actors and actresses came under her spell during their impressionable, training years, and the list of great dramatic stars—not dancers —of both stage and movies who sing her praises reads like a Who's Who in the American Theater.

She was also coaxed, reluctantly, to join a project organized by Tamiris and called the Dance Repertory Theater. Before it came into being in 1929, all modern dance units had separate managers, separate promotion and advertising expenses. Sunday evenings were the only nights open to them on Broadway, since shows played Mondays through Saturdays, and they'd fight each other for a free night. By getting together, they could engage a single manager, pool advertising costs, and even take an unused theater for a week instead of contracting for Sunday nights in a theater which often had permanent sets that could not be moved, except at hideous expense, for a recital.

It was all grudging. Martha hated collaboration. Tamiris, redheaded and radical, was bossy, even though she was the youngest. Doris and Charles were afraid that since "Denishawn had been organized to death" in their estimation, any kind of organization was dangerous. Doris also added, "I haven't much faith in Martha Graham. She's a snake if there ever was one." Behind the scenes temperaments flared, but the Dance Repertory Theater survived for two years after its first Broadway season in 1930. Dancers, of course, were not involved in exchanges from company to company. Each director zealously guarded his own brood from contamination by others, so that Graham dances and dancers remained isolated from Humphrey–Weidman dances and dancers. But still they shared in this repertory effort.

Modern dance had never had such good coverage by the press, especially with Martin and Watkins working hard to interest a still uncertain public in the new forms. Miss Watkins, just before she died at eighty-five in 1974, told me that many of the moderns would come to her and beg, on their knees, for special attention. She recalled that she was immune to their pleadings but wholeheartedly behind the cause of all dancers when they were at their best in their pioneering efforts.

Modern dance, in its starkest sense, did mirror the times. The Great Depression of the 1930s meant that jobs were scarce and many millions of people were starving. The unemployed sold apples and pencils on street corners. College graduates had no jobs to go to. There was no unemployment insurance, no old age security then. Blue Cross, Medicare, and Medicaid were uninvented. The Broadway theater nearly died because few people could afford tickets. The depression became worldwide. Abroad, people were turning to communism, to fascism, to any kind of "ism" that seemed to promise jobs.

Dance in America felt that it could not be escapist,
that it had to speak for the times. Doris had said that
ballet was much like the Sleeping Beauty herself—a girl
of sixteen who fell asleep and when she woke up one
hundred years later was still only sixteen and presumably no brighter. The moderns were going to dance
about adults and adult problems. No sugarcoatings.
Unrest, onstage and offstage. Many dancers, like Tamiris, joined other artists and intellectuals in moving
sharply to the left politically. They carried banners and
marched in the May Day parades, singing "Solidarity
Forever" and the "Internationale." Martha was furious
because many of her dancers, while performing with her
out of town, insisted on returning to New York for the
May Day march.

Martha, Doris, and Charles were liberals, not
leftists. But they did not shy away from the injustices of
the times. Doris, Charles, Tamiris, and, a bit later,
Germany's gift to American dance, Hanya Holm,
attacked current problems directly with their choreographies: *Lynch Town* (Weidman), *Trend* (Holm),
Adelante (Tamiris), *New Dance* (Humphrey). Martha was
more oblique or, one should say, more likely to distill
elements of conflict into something timeless, although
her *Immigrant* of the 1920s and *Chronicle* of the 1930s, a
long statement about the Spanish Civil War, were, for
her, fairly specific.

She was more likely to concentrate on abstracting
the essence of tragedy or ecstasy or conflict. Audiences
were shocked by a solo such as *Lamentation.* In polite
society a woman would dab a handkerchief to her eyes
at a funeral or, perhaps, bend her head forward.
Foreigners, with their strange customs, might wail or

War Theme (1941), like *Chronicle* and *Deep Song*, reflected
Martha Graham's concern with the Spanish Civil War.
It was a study, inspired by a poem of William Carlos
Williams'.

PHOTOGRAPH BY BARBARA MORGAN

even beat their breasts, but Americans? Heavens, no!
Martha wanted to show what happened when someone
was really bereft. She put herself into a body-tight tube
of purple jersey. At least she conformed to the colors of
mourning! It was like a shroud. It gave extension and
frightening contours to every body spasm. And there
were spasms, for Martha probed the very insides of a
being and brought to the surface visceral cramps and
aches and deep pain. Of course it was ugly, this
exposure of something that should be locked politely
within. But it was truthful.

It was powerful too, if you could accept it. I saw
Lamentation when I was a college student of about
eighteen. Martha was dancing a solo recital, and I can't
remember anything else clearly except *Lamentation*. I
thought it was silly. She didn't just bow her head in
sorrow, she went so far forward—I think she was sitting
on a bench—that her face was near her feet. Somebody
next to me said, "I wonder if she's looking to see if she
has athlete's foot!" We all thought it a very funny
remark. I had barely begun dance lessons at my
university (it was wholly extracurricular then, and boys
almost never dared study dance for fear of being called
"sissy"), and I wasn't beyond the dance exercise stage.
But *Lamentation*, with its indelible images, stuck in my
mind, and a year later, when my body was wiser in
dance, I replayed it in memory and was deeply moved
by it.

This was all so different from the conventions of
ballet. In *Giselle*, for example, when Giselle dies, her
young suitor holds her in his arms and weeps. But what
was happening to him inside? He had betrayed her
love, and he alone was to blame for her going insane, for

grabbing a sword to press against her heart, and for her ultimate death. Whatever the hero felt inside you never saw, only the surface conventions of sorrow. Martha in *Lamentation* showed you the total, agonized lamenting of that young suitor plus all those lovers—mothers, sisters, children, adults—all humans who had experienced loss and with it, unbearable anguish.

Although Ted Shawn pretended he never saw her recitals, he must have, for he couldn't wait to rip Martha's new dance approach to pieces. Miss Ruth didn't like it at all but chose to speak of it humorously. She would refer to Martha's technique as "the open crotch school of movement." Once when she saw her in the Greek classical drama *Electra*, starring the great actress Blanche Yurka, St. Denis described Martha's Dance of the Furies to a friend by saying, "and there was Martha doing split infinitives in the air while dear Blanche, as you might guess, just Yurked and Yurked."

Shawn couldn't laugh about it. In the 1930s he would maintain that if Martha herself or Martha and her company had performed in a university town, it killed that town for any other dance event for at least four years—until all the students had graduated, some of the professors had retired, and certain of the towns-people had died. With his company of men dancers, which he headed from 1933 to 1939, he would say that he would restore a community to the dance circuit after Martha had alienated everyone with her lamentations, anguishes, and ugliness.

There is always some truth in even the most outrageous allegations. When Shawn was spewing forth his diatribes in the mid-1930s, I remembered my own first reaction to *Lamentation*. I also heard nonbiased people of intelligence express bewilderment over Graham dances. They were not prepared for what they saw—to them a lamentation would probably be best expressed in dance by *The Dying Swan* of Pavlova.

By this time I had begun to study modern dance thoroughly in Graham, Humphrey, and Wigman techniques, and I used to say, "If I could arrange everything, modern dance would win over the public. To a city that had never had any modern dance, I'd send Charles Weidman first, because he uses a lot of pantomime and people at least can get the hang of what he is doing. Besides, he does comedy and people like to laugh.

"Next, I'd send Tamiris, because she does jazz dancing, even if it is in modern dance style, and because she's gorgeous and sexy and exciting even when she is calling upon the masses to rise. Next, as the audiences in that town began to catch on, I'd send Charles a second time, but this time with Doris, and then they'd see some abstract dances, like *Circular Descent* and *Pointed Ascent*, along with fairly understandable dances for men and women." (Humphrey–Weidman was the only one of the founding moderns to use men as well as women.)

"Next, Hanya would go, because her girls are the prettiest and most feminine." (Martha's girls were grim-faced automatons, really quite sexless.) "And then they'd be ready for Martha." I was never permitted to organize this crusade, but it wasn't a bad idea. My father, as a boy, had been taken to Wagner's *Parsifal* for his first opera experience. He never went to the opera again in his life. My first opera was *Carmen*—I got to Wagner much later—and I love opera. Innocent people who were introduced to modern dance by Martha in

her sledgehammer, unsmiling, angular period sometimes said to themselves, "If this is modern dance, no
more!"

But Martha was a pioneer, as her ancestors had
been. They had pressed into the wilderness with axe
and saw, plow and seed. She was pressing into a new
area of dance. She was at her own frontier. Indeed, in
1935 she made for herself a historic solo and called it
Frontier. It had an original score by Louis Horst, and for
the first time she departed from a barren stage; she had
a set. It was small and modest, but it had been done not
by a scene designer but by a sculptor, Isamu Noguchi.
(She continued to commission his art for her theater for
the next forty years.)

Martha's concept of décor for dance was that it be
structural rather than pictorial. Ballet, aside from
thrones or tables and chairs for a festive scene or a
Maypole with ribbons and similar "props," was set off
by a painted backdrop and painted side panels, which
might be columns or, perhaps, the ends of a wall or
branches in a forest. Martha wanted something three-
dimensional that would be part of the choreography.
Doris Humphrey got her three-dimensional, almost
architectural, effects from ramps, platforms, and boxes,
which could be arranged in all kinds of positions.
Martha's were to be sculptural. Noguchi's fence in
Frontier was an integral part of Martha's choreographic
designs for her body in repose, in advances, and in
retreats.

Later, Noguchi settings (and the settings of the
very few other designers she employed) would be more
elaborate. A twisted, uneven, sloping golden bed in
Night Journey would suggest not a royal resting place but,

in the heroine's memory, the site of a dire sin, an erotic torture rack. In another work a stone rampart would actually move as if to crush, conceal, protect, or imprison the heroine as she too moved along the inexorable course of tragedy.

The set for *Frontier* consisted of one section of a fence and two ropes. The dancer stood with one foot firmly planted on the earth and the other placed high on the top bar of the fence. Her torso rotated and as her head turned to scan the horizons, she smiled. It was the first time that Martha had discarded the mask-like face that Louis had insisted was a symbol of the highest age of theater, when actors wore masks and expressed themselves solely through movement and mime.

I was there and it was the most ravishing smile I have ever seen in my life. In that smile was mirrored the promise that a frontierswoman saw as she looked over a vast new land. It wasn't a frontierland with settlers and Indians, although my grandmother, who had gone by covered wagon to the Dakotas, might have read that into the dance, nor was it a frontier you could find in an atlas. It was the frontier you would find only on the chart of your own life-experience. It was the frontier that faced a girl or boy setting out to make the journey through life; it was the frontier of a bride or a mother-to-be or a soldier or an astronaut (even though they had not even been dreamed of then) or of a scientist or . . . of you and me. It was everyone's frontier, for Martha Graham was dancing *about* us as well as *for* us. This was not only a frontier but a threshold. With that smile, Martha Graham invited us to step forward into a new dance experience that would change the course of the theater for decades, perhaps centuries, to come.

Martha Graham and Erick Hawkins in *Night Journey*.
Isamu Noguchi's stylized golden bed was an integral
part of the choreography.

PHOTOGRAPH BY ARNOLD EAGLE

Letter to the World

Having failed in Tamiris's attempt to have them unite forces within the framework of the Dance Repertory Theater, the battling moderns allowed a few years to slip by before trying collaboration again. The second time, they had an umpire, not a tempestuous dancer, as their leader, and the setting was not a Broadway theater but a campus. Furthermore, they were not called upon to perform on the same program but simply to share the same facilities. The place was Bennington College in the Green Mountains of southern Vermont, a school founded in 1932 with an avant-garde program.

Martha Hill was the originator of the dance program at Bennington, which was to grow into one of the most famous dance festivals in the world. Robert D. Leigh, founder-president of this progressive women's college, gave quick, affirmative response to Miss Hill's suggestion that Bennington establish its own school of the dance and, in summer sessions, bring the great modern dance leaders to the campus. They would teach not only dancers but also physical education instructors, who could return to their institutions ready to spread the dance gospel in the field of higher education.

In 1934 the project got under way with Miss Hill and Mary Josephine Shelley, the latter in an administrative capacity, as directors. Both were colleagues at the University of Chicago at the time. John Martin was on the advisory board, and the faculty consisted of Hill, who taught basic modern technique, teaching methods, and elementary dance composition throughout the summer, and Graham, Humphrey, Weidman, and Holm, each with intensive, consecutive two-week courses.

Horst was there to teach music and choreography updated from preclassic dance forms, and Norman Lloyd, who subsequently composed major scores for modern dance, also taught music. Stagecraft was under the direction of Arch Lauterer, an important young scene designer. The enrollment the first year was about one hundred students, ranging in age from the teens to fifty and in girth from slender to buxom, all women (twelve men students enrolled in 1936 for Weidman's classes). After the first year there was a waiting list for applicants from almost every state and from Canada.

For the modern dance leaders, Bennington, in depression times, was heaven. Here was a plant, a place with buildings, which they could use without rental.

With Louis Horst at Bennington.

With theater and studios available and a workshop for stagecraft, it was possible to think about settings. Graham, with her sculptured sets, and Humphrey, with her boxes and ramps, began to extend their choreographies from bodies into architectural settings. The old National Guard armory in the town of Bennington was also used, and it was here that Holm presented her first major American creation, *Trend.* The depth of the armory made it possible for her to use many different paths for the exits and entrances essential to her choreographic plan.

Martha Hill, cool and smiling but tough, kept discipline, and Mary Jo, equally cool, smiling, and tough, kept peace when temperaments started to flare. The stars were not fond of one another, Humphrey and Weidman (partners) excluded. The acolytes of each stayed apart. Humphrey commented on Graham's temper and temperament more than once, and Graham and Holm, somewhere along the line, reached the point where they would, if walking along the same street in Bennington or New York, cross the road to avoid the necessity of either greeting or snubbing.

Bennington was a little clique-ish. It was the core of modern dance and it looked down on nearby Jacob's Pillow in Lee, Massachusetts, where Ted Shawn had established his summer headquarters in 1933, as the stand of the old guard and reactionary dance. Shawn never went to Bennington, although his men dancers sneaked up there to look at the opposition and, as in the case of the highly intellectual, nonconforming Foster Fitz-Simons of the Shawn Men Dancers, sometimes responded enthusiastically to the great creative bursts at Bennington. Shawn, however, cowed most of the others

as he held court at his dining-room table in the old
farmhouse and vilified both the ballet, for its reactionary status and its European base, and the moderns,
for daring to go beyond where he had led.

Miss Ruth, however, was invited to Bennington.
Although she had been unhappy about the rebellions in
Denishawn, she never became the symbol of tyranny
that Shawn had become. She attended a performance
and was later escorted by Martha to the town restaurant where everyone gathered after performances. As
she entered, the students looked at her curiously and
then spontaneously rose and applauded her. The
breach was healed, and Miss Ruth was acknowledged
as the "mother" or at least the "ancestress" of modern
dance.

It was at Bennington in 1936 that I first saw Erick
Hawkins dance. He was a member of the newly
organized Ballet Caravan, founded by Lincoln Kirstein
to explore the talents of American choreographers,
composers, designers, and dancers in the field of ballet.
It was odd that a ballet company should make its debut
in what can be described as a hotbed of modern dance,
but its all-American goals made it at least an acceptable
curiosity. Hawkins met Martha that summer. The next
summer he choreographed his first ballet, *Showpiece*, for
the Ballet Caravan, and began to study modern dance
with Graham. In 1938 he joined the Graham company
as the first male dancer in the erstwhile all-girl group.
Eventually, he and Martha were married after the
couple had shared an apartment for a while. Sometime
later, John Martin said to me, "Well, Martha's made
peace with her Puritan ancestors at last."

Erick first danced with Martha in *American Docu-*

ment, which was premiered at the Bennington Armory in the summer of 1938. It was her most theatrical production to date, with a setting by Arch Lauterer, costumes by Edythe Gilfond (previously Martha had designed her own), and music by Ray Green. In addition to the score, the work employed a narrator speaking excerpts from American documents and from the Bible. Erick, tall, handsome, muscular, perhaps a bit wooden in his newfound modern dance guise, was a success. Martha took on a new femininity, and her girls seemed less stark than they had.

There had been, of course, men dancers at Denishawn, and Doris Humphrey's partnership with Weidman made it essential for Charles to have male dancers to work with in the Humphrey–Weidman group. Tamiris followed suit and engaged Daniel Nagrin as her partner. (Like Martha, she eventually married her leading man.) Hanya Holm was the last of the leading lady moderns to give up an all-girl group. Ballet, of course, required men dancers by the very nature of its repertory. Once the period of "travesty," in the late nineteenth and early twentieth centuries, in which ballerinas performed male roles, was over, the male in dance, starting with Vaslav Nijinsky of Diaghilev's Ballets Russes, and Pavlova's first partner in America, the Bolshoi's Mikhail Mordkin, began his ascendancy. It would lead, in the 1960s and '70s, to male superstars —Erik Bruhn, Rudolf Nureyev, and Edward Villella in ballet; José Limón, Merce Cunningham, and Paul Taylor in modern dance—almost edging out the female stars. Martha, as usual in the vanguard of the dance, did much to further the stature of the male in American dance.

Martha exerted an almost hypnotic power over her girls. *Time* magazine had referred to her and her *Frontier* in its customary smart-aleck way with a picture caption that said, "High Priestess Martha Graham and her surrealist fence act." Martha never liked being thought of as a priestess. She expected to be obeyed but not blindly imitated. Her Bennington students, enthralled, copied her look and her mannerisms, just as movie fans in the 1920s would come out of a Gloria Swanson matinee with, seemingly, more teeth than they had when they went in. Thus, even a red-haired, freckle-faced, round-cheeked girl who looked nothing like Martha would lower her eyelids in order to appear "deep" and mysterious, suck in her cheeks in an effort to arrive at Martha's sculptured facial contours, pull her hair back severely, and, given half a chance, lurch along the streets of Bennington in a series of contractions and releases.

Martha herself carried contractions and releases into her own offstage life. John Butler, a onetime Graham dancer who became a choreographer of international acclaim, told me that once when he lived near Graham he could look out his window across a courtyard and see her at her desk. He said, "It was really funny. Martha, sitting, would contract her arm and shoulder to pick up her pen, do a release while she was thinking what she was going to write, and then contract furiously as she began to scribble."

Even later, Robert Cohan, a leading Graham dancer, said, "You should see Martha in the A & P. She goes down the aisles the way she crosses the stage!"

But Martha, vivid and original, could be both imitated and caricatured. She could even poke fun at

herself while satirizing the foibles of others. Occasionally in her solo pieces she would touch upon satire and
comedy, but she never ripped into it until she created
Every Soul Is a Circus, her first major comic effort. It was
about an empty-headed woman who fancied herself as
empress of the arena of her life. Martha caricatured her
with ruthless gestural comments about her uselessness
and, at the same time, distorted her own basic technique sufficiently to make you laugh at the movements
as well as the mover. In my 1939 review in the New
York *Herald Tribune* I wrote that Martha Graham is
"the Beatrice Lillie of the dance and she's been hiding it
from us all these years." The reference was to the great
comedienne who had generations of theatergoers
rocking with laughter at her British-accented humor in
musicals, revues, movies, radio, and recordings.

In the summer of 1940, the year after *Circus* was
done on Broadway, Martha presented at Bennington
the first version of what was to prove to be one of her
major creations, her first dance-drama, her first real
biography in dance, her first fairly elaborate (for those
dance days) production, and her clearest statement of
what she really meant about "the inner man" and "the
interior landscape." It was called *Letter to the World*, and
it was a dual biography, a portrait of the outer being
and the inner self of the New England poet Emily
Dickinson. The music was by Hunter Johnson, the
setting by Arch Lauterer, the costumes by Gilfond. The
narrator, one of the two "Emilys" in the work, spoke
lines from Dickinson poems. The piece was given in the
small college theater, not in the armory.

Martha's idea was to reveal the "true," as she
conceived it, Emily Dickinson. This would not be like

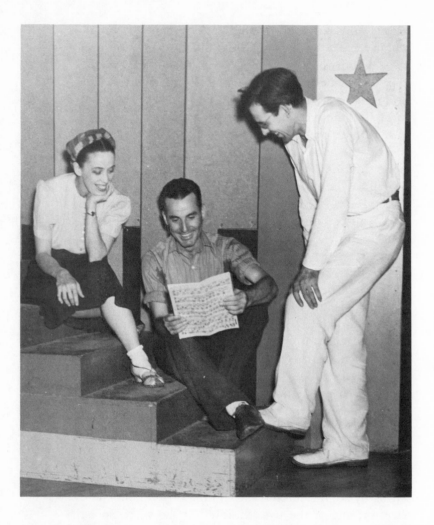

Backstage at Bennington, with Hunter Johnson (center) and Arch Lauterer (right), composer and designer for *Letter to the World*.

an "exposé" in a sensation-seeking magazine; it would
be a choreographic probing. Martha, who had read and
reread everything that Emily had ever written and
everything written about her, was certain that the real
Emily was not the well-bred, polite, conventional lady
that her neighbors saw. There was a hidden inner self
with its own "interior landscape," which would be quite
distinct from the "outer landscape," the geographical
landscape surrounding the Dickinson home. Neighbors
and townsfolk lived in the outer landscape, but Emily's
secret landscape was peopled with figures utterly free in
their responses to life and death, ecstasy and fantasy.
These were mortals and immortals consorting together.

One Emily, the speaker, was played by a Graham
dancer, Jean Erdman, who took precise steps on her
exits and entrances, who paused and stood with dignity,
who comported herself in a manner that would not be
amiss in a strict Puritan setting. She spoke words from
the Dickinson poems, and Martha, as the inner, hidden
Emily, gave substance and form to those words. Sometimes Martha was dressed in blue, evoking romance on
a starlit night; sometimes in red, for passion; or again,
in multicolors as she hopped around, tied her foot to a
scarf and pulled the foot ear-high as she lurched
happily as "the little tippler leaning against the sun."
For Martha, and for most in her audience, there was
little question as to which Emily actually wrote the
heart-searching poems that touched the hearts of read-
ers everywhere. It was, of course, the inner Emily.
Martha introduced her to us and took us in theatrical
fantasy into that interior landscape where Emily Dickinson had, most certainly, penned her "Letter to the
World."

The decade of the 1930s had been great years for

Martha. She had found valuable assistance in the
Dance Repertory Theater, despite its short life; at
Bennington; and at the Neighborhood Playhouse where
she profoundly influenced actors for stage and screen.
Her impact on acting was especially highlighted when
she was engaged to stage the movement and the dances
for *The Rape of Lucrece*, starring one of the most
celebrated actresses of the day, Katharine Cornell, who
became her lifelong friend and devoted admirer.

During this decade she was awarded a John Simon
Guggenheim fellowship, which permitted her to travel
to the Southwest and to Mexico, an area that never
ceased to fascinate her and which inspired many of her
most successful pieces, *Primitive Mysteries* and *El Penitente*
among them.

It was the period of her most fruitful collaboration
with Louis as a composer and one of great pride in his
independent achievements, such as his founding of *The
Dance Observer*, a magazine devoted exclusively to modern dance, which was published from 1934 until Louis's
death in 1964. The *Observer* critics naturally reviewed
Graham performances, but no favoritism was shown, for
Louis would not permit anything but absolute honesty
of opinion. Martha got some rough, although always
respectful, treatment in the pages of the *Observer*.

Mrs. Franklin D. Roosevelt also invited her to
dance for a small group of guests at the White House.
The President's wife was interested in the arts as well as
the humanities, and the Graham performance marked
the first time a dancer had been asked to the White
House in a long time. The publicity brought Martha
and modern dance to the attention of the general
public.

"Dear March, come in!" Graham and Merce Cunningham in *Letter to the World*, 1940.

PHOTOGRAPH BY BARBARA MORGAN

The '30s, choreographically, had peaked for Martha in her initial experiments in the great *Frontier* solo and in *Primitive Mysteries*, perhaps a partial transference of the Catholic mass that Lizzie had taken her to see and a distillation of those Indian ceremonials she had studied in the Southwest. Martha played the primitive Virgin (Christian-Indian-ageless), and her dancers, moving onstage and off in silence except for the sound of the firm, purposeful tread of bare feet, were the celebrants in this danced ritual divided into Hymn to the Virgin, Crucifixus, and Hosanna.

With the 1940s, Martha began her true "theater" of dance. She developed a gallery of portraits (inner and outer as in her two Emilys), began to win over those she had previously scared off with her sledgehammer tactics, and began to see her influence spread not only to her pupils but even, of all places, to the Broadway theater, where her theories on the communication of inner passions could be adapted to musical-comedy dance.

It was in the 1940s also that a more universally significant trend in dance began to develop swiftly and healthily. This was the integration of the races within a theatrical troupe. Historically, there had been occasional examples of integration—Juba, a black tap dancer, was the star of an all-white company as far back as 1850. Now, a century after Juba, black dancers were participating in an increasing number of dance events. There were blacks in the Federal Dance Project of the depression years, and Ted Shawn's Jacob's Pillow Dance Festival, from the late 1930s on, never failed to have black artists on the stage each season.

Blacks and Asian Americans in increasing numbers

entered modern dance companies, Broadway shows (other than the usual black revues or musicals with a black specialty dancer), and grand opera. Classical ballet was about the last to engage blacks, although Asian Americans came early. Martha was among the first to open her company to all races, and, indeed, black dancers and those of Asian heritage would soon become key figures in her troupe even to the point of assuming historic Graham roles in the 1970s when Martha retired as a dancer.

Appalachian Spring

Martha had been an adult at the time of the First World War, but in California the conflict had seemed remote. The most pressing aspect of the war had been whether Ted Shawn would get his weekend leaves from officers' training camp to allow him to teach at Denishawn.

By the time of World War II, however, Martha had become not only an adult with profound convictions but a choreographer whose duty it was to respond to the times in which she lived. In the 1930s she had touched upon the tragedy of the Spanish Civil War. But in the 1940s a new war had come close not only to her but to her ancient heritage, her American pride. She had, of course, paid tribute to that heritage in *American Document* and in an abstraction, *Frontier*. She had celebrated her first American heroine, Emily Dickinson, in *Letter to the World*, and she had paid lovely homage to the rituals of the Indian-Hispanic-American Southwest in *El Penitente*. But with the war against Hitlerism, despite the fact that she separated art and personal response from anything suggesting the political scene, she became patriotic without being political.

She did a dance called *Land Be Bright*. Her intentions were good, but the piece failed. She closed the show and put it out of her mind. *Salem Shore*, a solo, was considerably better, in fact, a modest success. In it she recalled that curious sense of contented loneliness that seacoast New Englanders experience as they stand and scan the horizon, the only apparent boundary to the ageless sea. More than that, she seemed to evoke the olden days when New England maidens looked to that empty sea with a silent prayer that their sailor lovers or husbands would give that horizon a new silhouette, the promise of return.

But the triumph was *Appalachian Spring*. Commissioned by the Elizabeth Sprague Coolidge Foundation in the Library of Congress (Mrs. Coolidge was a generous patron of the arts), it was first presented in the theater at the library. The score, which Martha commissioned, was by Aaron Copland. It subsequently won a Pulitzer Prize and became, perhaps, the most popular and oft-played score by an American composer. For her designs, Martha again engaged Isamu Noguchi. Noguchi was a Nisei, an American-born Japanese, a member of a group of Americans who suffered deeply and were treated disgracefully during the war simply because of

their Japanese heritage. The piece was an instant
success and has remained the most popular ballet (to
use a classical term, now accepted for any full-scale
dance work) in the Graham repertory.

Martha, who played the role of the Bride in
Appalachian Spring, was just fifty when it was first
performed in 1944. Her age didn't matter. Martha was
never a young bride in fact or in spirit. Her Bride in
Spring was a distillation of the radiance, the hope, the
dedication to husband and husbandry of the pioneer
wife. Martha could evoke this from her very being, for
her own forebears were pioneering women in the still
wild Appalachians and she herself was ever one to
hearken to what she often called "the ancestral footsteps," her way of expressing her link with the past.

The setting consisted of the side of a house (which
the Husbandman stroked as he made his entrance), a
front porch with a near-skeletal rocking chair (as spare
as a pioneer woman), a bench by the side of the house, a
portion of fence, and a sloping rock on which the
visiting Preacher could stand tall above his flock.

Here, there are husband-wife love, the suggestion
of a baby, the beckoning of a further frontier, lonesome-
ness and adventure, pride in building, joy coupled with
incredible self-discipline. He stands by his fence looking
over his domain. She watches shyly. Sometimes, she will
do a dance of prayer, of hope, by herself, just as he, by
himself, seems to go forth beyond the farm. The visiting
Pioneer Woman looks ever to the horizon, urging the
husband on, while the wife, mute but concerned,
literally caresses the threshold with her body. The
revivalist visits, followed by the pious maidens of his
congregation. Ecstatically, he promises blessings and

Appalachian Spring, 1944. Erick Hawkins as the Husbandman and Graham (seated) as the Bride, May O'Donnell (right) as the Pioneer Woman.

PHOTOGRAPH BY ARNOLD EAGLE

hope and, with gestures resembling thunderbolts, warns of hellfire and damnation for the sinner.

There are the courtesies extended to visiting neighbors, the rocking of a babe in arms, a flash of a carefree dance in which the man and his wife forget the world and cherish each other with linked arms, warm embraces, or in that glorious moment when the dominant male sweeps his tiny bride off her feet and swings her into dream-space (perhaps as Dr. Graham ran upstairs with his diminutive Jenny in his arms). All, all of this happening—one cannot believe it is the stage of make-believe—amid the lovely sweetness of an Appalachian spring when America was young.

Martha danced the role of the Bride well into her sixties, when she relinquished it to younger dancers. Once, however, on a special occasion, I urged her to dance it again. She said she was too old. I retorted that she had never been young in a girlish sense. She smiled and danced it divinely for an audience that cheered her to the rafters. I remembered, as I watched her, what the great actress Jane Cowl is reported to have said earlier in the century when she was criticized for announcing that she would play Juliet in *Romeo and Juliet*: "You have to be forty to know the wonder of being fourteen." Martha was, indeed, the Bride.

With *Appalachian Spring*, legions of anti-Grahamites were completely captivated. Emily Coleman, the brilliant, and sometimes remorseless, dance and music critic for *Newsweek*, had bowed to no one in her appreciation of Martha's great influence on dance and the theater itself, but she had never personally liked the Graham dances. "What the hell's romantic about a dirty, bare foot being shoved into someone's face?" In *Spring*,

Martha was shod. Emily Coleman, though occasionally cringing when dirty soles were hoisted, became a convert.

Martha did not carry *Spring* alone. Erick Hawkins had his best role as the husband. Tall, strapping, somewhat gauche, stern-featured, he looked for all the world like what was subsequently to be described as "a male chauvinist," the head of the house, the rooster among hens.

One of Martha's greatest dance discoveries—he had already made a tremendous impact as March in *Letter to the World*—Merce Cunningham danced the part of the Preacher with a hypnotic force that mesmerized not only the congregation onstage but audiences as well. A young man who moved with the sinewy strength of an animal, Merce possessed a good deal of the fierce intensity that characterized Martha herself. When he rebelled against her, as she had against Denishawn, he became the undisputed leader, as he remains in the '70s, of the avant-garde in dance.

May O'Donnell, long-limbed, firm-jawed, impressive of stance, was the Pioneer Woman, and even little Yuriko (a major Graham soloist) was a force as the sweetest, most devout, and appealingly vulnerable of the worshipful maidens.

Martha Graham was clearly more than a controversial innovator—the 1940s cleared that up once and for all. She was a great choreographer. She'd had some doubts about that a few years before. So did others. The critic Walter Sorrell in his book *Hanya Holm, The Biography of an Artist*, states that Martha dominated Bennington and, indeed, the whole modern dance scene not as a choreographer but as "the most glamorous

figure and the strongest performer." Humphrey looked
upon Graham as highly artificial, "but not silly—a
hothouse flower, intensely feminine, not a flaming
flower but a night-blooming thing with a faint exotic
perfume." Mary Watkins recalled in 1974 that in first
reviewing Martha she had found her dances "a little
ridiculous." Her initial responses were not very cordial,
"although they improved when I found what she was
aiming for. . . . But of all those moderns it was Doris
who was the choreographer."

Martha herself couldn't have agreed more. "Doris
is really the choreographer," she said. "I'm a dancer.
Doris knows how to put a dance together. I don't." Still,
she had always gone ahead with making dances, partly
as an expedient, because she wanted to dance something she cared about and only she could come up with
themes that inspired her as a dancer. The public, with
Spring, disagreed with this premise. They accepted her
as a great choreographer. She began to think they
might be right.

This by no means indicated that Martha would be
a compromiser. She wasn't about to pay any more
nostalgic visits to the Appalachians. Her next work, in
1946, was one of the most difficult to understand of any
that she had ever done. It was called *Dark Meadow*. It
did indeed leave people in the dark.

The theme, as far as I was concerned, seemed to be
man's search for assurance of his own immortality. The
work was like an ancient ritual, the participants
engaged in a ceremony so old that they had forgotten its
meaning but still believed in its magical efficacy. Here,
Martha had a section that she designated as "the
ancestral footsteps." She seemed to be saying that if we

have a past we must have a future, that the echoes of the past will echo through the today and into the tomorrows. There were symbols, such as a blade of wheat, suggesting fertility of the earth; the Cross, promising everlasting life; a bowl containing a cloth dipped either into the blood of sacrifice or the blood of life. There was a beautifully erotic dance for men and women that seemed to sing—for muscles as well as voices can sing—of love. The closing episode was called "the ecstasy of the flowering branch." It was impossible to say what it meant in a literal sense, but one sensed it was a statement of a recurrent Garden of Eden, where life had begun.

At the premiere at the National Theater in New York, one of the ushers fled to the ladies' room shortly after the public was seated and the curtain rose. Isadora Bennett, Miss Graham's press representative, could not brook indifference by anyone. She pursued the usher and asked her why she had left. The young woman said she didn't understand the dance and, indeed, hated what she had seen. Miss Bennett recognized in the usher a fellow Irishwoman and suggested to her that what she didn't understand was the mysterious, magical work of "the little people." The usher agreed that she did believe in leprechauns and that in dark meadows at home in Ireland the little people did, in fact, hold their fairy ceremonies. With Miss Bennett's personal incantation working, the usher returned to her aisle. She wept with delight and secret understanding and never missed another performance.

When my own review of *Dark Meadow* appeared in the New York *Herald Tribune* Martha called me and said, "So that's what it was about!" Martha wasn't

In *Dark Meadow*, 1946, Graham created a mysterious ritual.

pulling a hoax on her audience, it was simply that she never verbalized her works. She let instinct guide her, and she did, as she preached, give substance to things felt.

When *Dark Meadow* was danced in Rome a decade later, the Italian audience booed. Martha did not bring the curtain down. The company finished. She ordered them to stand there for a curtain call. She instructed them not to bow. Just to stand. They did. In dignity. At the end of the program, the Graham dancers received an ovation.

Iva Kitchell, a popular dance satirist of the day, added Martha to her list of parodies. Audiences roared at her ballerina who fell on her face, her bacchanale-at-the-opera dancer who got tangled up in scarves and ewers and garlands, her Spanish dancer who tried to manipulate castanets and roses and daggers all at once. They howled with delight at her new *Soul in Search*, in which a harried woman in Graham-like dress crawled about the stage crying "seek, search, seek, search!" as she tore through "fallow fields" and meadows. Kitchell never satirized anything she couldn't do well herself, and she was so good at Graham technique in her parody that Louis Horst, escorting Martha to a benefit show where Kitchell danced, laughed appreciatively and said, "Martha, hire that girl; she's better than some you've got in the company." Martha smiled. She didn't laugh.

This year, 1946, also brought *Cave of the Heart* and the beginning of her continuing cycle of dance-dramas suggested by the myths and dramas of the classical world. *Cave* was about Medea, the sorceress of Colchis whose husband, Jason, a Thessalonian king, was unfaithful. Consumed with jealousy and fired by the need for revenge, Medea killed the other woman with a poisoned crown and slew her own children, presenting their bodies to her husband.

Martha stressed that her *Cave of the Heart* was not a dance chronicle of Medea but of "one like Medea." In other words, Martha was again distilling essences, and she was addressing herself to the Medea lurking in every woman, to the element of jealousy that destroys everything it touches. She had at first called her work *The Serpent Heart*, but apparently that was too precise for her liking, although the core of the piece was a solo for Medea in which she seems to devour a red snake, then spews it out as if her own heart had become a poisonous serpent.

Night Journey was about Jocasta, another doomed queen of the ancient Greek drama. The fates had decreed that Jocasta, unknowingly, would marry her own son and bear him children. Martha's fairly long dance-drama took place in what she called "the instant of awareness." In other words, her ballet wasn't chronological. It opened as Jocasta learned the awful truth. What followed were episodes that flashed through her mind in tormenting remembrance.

The key movement in *Night Journey* was a remarkably virtuosic action very probably never done before in the millions of years that dancing has existed. Certainly it was totally unknown to classical ballet or to any form of ethnic dance (dance forms evolved by a culture—Spanish, East Indian, or Japanese—and not by a dance school or an individual). It consisted of—in a quick sequence that seemed almost a simultaneous act—a head-high kick as the body began to lean forward in a perilous response to the pull of gravity while the lowering leg reached out to carry the body into a split on the floor.

Later I asked Martha how she had conceived such an incredibly spectacular and dramatically powerful movement. "I felt that when Jocasta became aware of the enormity of her crime, a cry from the lips would not be enough. It had to be a cry from the loins themselves, the loins which had committed sin." Indeed, the body opened in that terrible moment. You did not hear a cry. You saw it.

With *Errand into the Maze*, Martha turned to the legend of the Minotaur and the Cretan Labyrinth. Again, Graham was not concerned with a literal telling of the story of Theseus who was sent to kill the monster-bull in that labyrinth where he had devoured so many Greek youths and maidens sacrificed to him. Martha's labyrinth was the maze of the human heart. Theseus was not a Greek hero but you or I. In the Graham telling, it was a statement that each of us, sometime in his life, must do battle with the creature of fear—the insecurity or self-doubts that beset us all and will destroy us if we do not destroy them. *Errand* had a cast of two: the woman, symbolic of Theseus or any potential victim of terror, and the monster. The battle was vivid and terrifying and, at the close, when the liberated figure races along the maze of curves and twists, which are indicated by a long movable white plastic cord rather like a tape measure by the yard, and reaches an exit and freedom through two huge props resembling a giant wishbone, we all sigh with intense relief.

These and other Graham creations of the 1940s

also were the product of Martha's historic collabora-
tions with some of the greatest of contemporary com-
posers. In addition to Copland and one last work by
Louis Horst (*El Penitente*), some of her composers were
Paul Hindemith, William Schuman, Samuel Barber,
Hunter Johnson, Gian Carlo Menotti, Carlos Chávez,
Paul Nordoff, Darius Milhaud, Robert McBride, and
Norman Dello Joio.

Dello Joio composed the score for Martha's non-
Greek, non-dramatic masterpiece *Diversion of Angels*, one
of the first dances she did in which she herself did not
dance. It was, and remains, a gloriously joyful abstract
ballet in which beautiful people move lyrically, play-
fully, romantically, innocently with the sweetness of
angels. It joined *Appalachian Spring* as one of the few
Graham creations that bewildered nobody and delighted everybody.

Diversion of Angels had its world premiere in the
Palmer Auditorium of Connecticut College for Women
at New London, Connecticut. This was the opening
year of the American Dance Festival, and it is important because it was Bennington, both school and
festival, reborn after World War II in a new place.
Martha Hill was again the guiding genius. Martha was
there, so too was Doris, this time not as a dancer but as
the artistic adviser and chief choreographer for José
Limón (the most distinguished product of the Humphrey–Weidman school and company) and his group. A
new modern dance generation was making itself felt.

José, Merce Cunningham, Erick Hawkins, and
their contemporaries had no hatred for Denishawn or
for St. Denis and Shawn. They were curious about these
two historical figures. Some of them were not quite

convinced that they should swallow whole what Martha, Doris, Charles, and Louis said about the Denishawners. José went to Jacob's Pillow, where Ted Shawn had a much bigger festival than New London, danced there, and was captivated by Shawn. Miss Ruth swept into New London and enchanted everyone. Shawn came to give a single lecture and restrained himself, with great difficulty, from saying that he had invented dancing. He heaped praise on Martha, Doris, Charles, and their successors. After his lecture in what he called "the enemy camp," Doris went backstage, put her arms around him, and with her usual forthrightness said, "Ted, I had forgotten how much we all learned from you. I'm ashamed." The breach was healing.

Martha, with *Spring* and longer New York engagements (not just single recitals) plus national tours, was becoming famous. She even appeared as a mystery guest on a very popular radio program that gave prizes to listeners who could identify voices speaking short sentences with clues to their identity in each weekly change of script. Since advertising profits went to a charity, Martha agreed.

Martha and Erick, who were married in 1948, enjoyed not a peaceful relationship but an ardent and tempestuous one. Erick was in the same situation as the young Ted Shawn who had had his ego problems with the older and more famous St. Denis. Before and after marriage, Erick was always the lesser. Martha permitted him to choreograph—*John Brown*, a solo with narration, was his first work—and she made dances especially for him, one being *Eye of Anguish*, suggested by Shakespeare's *King Lear*. Nothing he himself did and no major work created just for him was successful. Erick took a strong interest in the company, worked hard to make it a success, and relieved Martha of many administrative problems, but there was one fact he overlooked: the entire enterprise consisted of but one person, Martha Graham. The Graham company was exactly what Miss Ruth had defined her elaborate costumes and draperies to be: "An extension of my body movements into space," and the Graham dancers were continuations of the genius of Martha beyond her own body.

Around the World

The 1950s launched Martha's eventual conquest of the world's theater. The decade began, however, with disaster, with an antagonistic press and a serious injury to Graham herself at the very start of a European engagement in 1950. Europe, presumably, had been prepared for Martha Graham and America's modern dance on an esthetic-intellectual level by Martha's newest patroness, the Baroness Bethsabée de Rothschild, a member of the French branch of the historic banking family. In 1949 the Baroness had written and published a book called *La Danse Artistique aux U.S.A.* It was a scholarly, well-researched, beautifully illustrated book about America's modern dance movement. Martha, understandably, was well represented in it.

Still, when the Graham dancers went to the
Baroness's homeland in 1950, they were not well
received. The French preferred ballet, and though they
enjoyed novelty, they preferred their own brand. Lincoln Kirstein once dismissed French ballet by saying it
was nothing more than "the art of dressmaking."

Martha did not have time to dig in and fight for
approval in Paris, for she tore a ligament in her knee in
performance and could not continue. She was in pain
and in a rage. Erick pulled together a program without
her, an almost impossible feat since Graham herself was
what the company was all about. Martha was first and
foremost a dancer and her interest in her company,
which she trained superbly, was as a background for
herself. Twenty years later this total identification of
herself with the act of performing would come close to
destroying both her legend and her life.

The rest of the Paris run was canceled. They
moved on to London. Martha tried out the leg. She
simply couldn't dance. She was in despair and she took
out her frustration on everyone. There are two conflict-
ing reports on what happened in London. One published version is that Erick suggested canceling London
and that Martha objected violently. The more logical
story, in my opinion, is the one that was told to me by
the late Jean Rosenthal, lighting designer for Graham
productions and the most brilliant lighting artist of the
American theater in that period. Jean said, "Erick was
naturally trying to salvage the season, but he made one
great mistake. He not only suggested that the company
finish the engagement, he gave Martha the impression
that he felt she wasn't necessary. He probably didn't
mean it, but that's the way it came out. I couldn't even

begin to describe what Martha said and did. You wouldn't believe it. It was terrifying!" Whatever happened, that was the end, right there, of the Graham-Hawkins marriage. They remained together professionally for a short period but a divorce was later obtained.

Martha came back home and went almost immediately to New Mexico. She stayed with friends who respected her need for solitude combined with subtle attentiveness. Later she told me that she thought she might never dance again. The knee was a mess. The doctors she had been to disagreed on what to do about it. "Some thought I must have an operation," she said. "I refused. I won't have violation done to my body. I just waited and hoped, but then I found a marvelous young doctor in Albuquerque. He said an operation would be wrong. And he told me that I knew more about the body than any doctor. He said something like 'I'll tell you exactly what is torn and where. I'll give you the diagnosis and what needs to be repaired and you decide the treatments.' I did. It was lifting weights. I started with very little weights. I got to where I could put a typewriter in a sling and lift it with my leg. When I was able to lift twenty-five pounds, I was healed."

In subsequent years, many dancers who have experienced troubles with the knee—the most complex and fragile joint in the dancer's body and, in many ways, the most essential—would come to Martha with their woes. She'd talk to them all, even those she did not know personally, and tell them what she did and how long it took and how it felt. She wouldn't act as a doctor, of course; it was simply dancer-to-dancer dialogue that makes sense only to dancers. Dancers seem to be their own best therapists.

The next time that Martha danced it was especially for me. For some seasons I had been conducting
what I called a "Dance Laboratory," programs of
interview-demonstrations at the Young Men's and
Young Women's Hebrew Association at Ninety-second
Street and Lexington Avenue in New York City. The
"Y," as it was known to the world of dance and dancers,
was called the Dance Center of New York in the 1940s
and '50s. It had classes in modern dance, and under its
education director, Dr. William Kolodney, one of the
greatest friends modern dance ever had, the doors of the
"Y" were open to dancers who could not afford
Broadway theaters and whose programs were worthy of
more than studio performances in old loft buildings.

The lovely Kaufmann Auditorium was made
available at cost to dancers and to experimenting
choreographers. There were choreographic workshops
out of which came major choreographic talents, and the
"Y" itself sponsored dance auditions and gave the
winners concerts onstage, all expenses paid. My own
Dance Laboratory series, consisting of six to eight
programs per season, lasted for a decade as I tried to
guide audiences behind the scenes to discover artists of
the dance and what they thought and how they worked.

With great stars I would do, say, The Art of the
Ballerina, or Music and Dance, or a series such as Sex
as a Dance Motivation, or Dancing and Religion, or the
Negro in the Dance.

When Martha appeared at the Dance Laboratory
the eight hundred-plus-seat theater was always sold out.
Fans came from as far away as Maine to attend one of
these Sunday matinees.

George Balanchine brought stars of the New York

City Ballet to the little stage and choreographed right before our eyes. Jerome Robbins, with a full company of dancers, did one act from his ballet *The Age of Anxiety*, and then took it apart, dissected it for the audience, and explained in detail how he had fashioned it.

When Martha came that time after her terrible accident, the program fell on an Easter Sunday. She danced magnificently and the audience stood and cheered. Not long afterward she telephoned me and asked if I would be continuing my Dance Laboratory series again in the fall. I said I would. She said, "May I dance for you again at the 'Y'?" Could she! I couldn't have been more excited. "Is there some time in late November when you'll be having a program?" Yes, there would be. "I should like to dance there at that time. I was reborn as a dancer last Easter Sunday. May I return to make my Thanksgiving?"

Martha could be like that. So sweet, so loving, so thoughtful, even deeply romantic and almost sentimental, yet the same woman could make an eruption of Vesuvius seem like a mild summer shower.

In 1954 she returned to Europe. There was no triumph in London. She made only a dent. The older critics found her pretentious. Dancing should be attractive and that's that. But a young critic, Richard Buckle, thought otherwise and said so. He said she was simply magnificent. Martha was not alone in being subjected to British disdain. St. Denis and Duncan, on their initial tries, were dismissed as novelties. Miss Ruth was referred to simply as "a performer." Because she did not use toe shoes she could not, in many a British mind, be classified as "a dancer." (Eventually Graham was to conquer the British so thoroughly that they established an academy founded on the Graham technique.)

Her return to Paris was a smashing success. The Baroness Bethsabée's mother saw to it that all the "right" Parisians were involved in the Graham season, and Martha herself was heaped with honors. Italy was not appreciative, but the Scandinavians were enchanted—some rugged soul bicycled all the way down from his home north of the Arctic Circle to see her in Stockholm. Vienna, as it had at the turn of the century with St. Denis and Duncan, treated Martha with the honor and respect due an artist of towering accomplishment.

The U.S. State Department was informed, through its European ambassadors, that it had a valuable and prestigious commodity in Martha Graham. Martha was surprised to find that the long-despised and disparaged modern dance should be deemed to have any popular appeal to persons in high quarters. But whatever American officials thought about the values of culture in general or modern dance in particular, they were aware that in almost any country other than America art was considered a national resource and the artist an individual of the highest importance. During World War II a Soviet ballerina or premier danseur carried travel permits equal to those of an army general. Europe looked upon the arts as a necessity, while the United States, officially at least, thought of it as a luxury, and a rather suspicious one at that. Countries as small as Denmark, and even municipalities, such as the German cities, allocated tax funds to state theaters presenting drama, opera, and ballet. But the richest country in the world, the United States of America, provided not one penny to the arts until 1954, when it established its Cultural Exchange Program (now called the Cultural Presentations Program).

Just before this new program was instituted I asked a senator if he would support federal funding of the arts. "Privately, I believe in it. But good God! if my constituents thought that I had approved legislation to use their tax money for pink toe shoes, I'd never be reelected!" This was the common fear of almost all legislators at the time. So when the first funding came it was for export, not to support the arts at home. It was almost as if the government were saying, "You and I know it's foolish, but those people overseas like arty things and it's good propaganda for us."

The Cultural Exchange Program was an instant success. The first American artist to go out under the State Department banner was José Limón. He was sent with his company to South America. A U.S. citizen of Mexican birth, part Indian and part Spanish, Limón could speak the Spanish tongue wherever he went. He was virile, noble, a brilliant dancer, and a perfect diplomat. Ticket prices, by American government orders, were kept at a modest level, but José, on his own, gave free performances to thousands of workers in open-air stadiums in South America. The experiment was a great success.

Martha went to Asia the following year, in 1955, and the reports that came back from embassies and consulates were that she had done more good for America than all the diplomats and dollars that had been sent to keep Far Eastern nations pro-American.

In Indonesia an anti-American newspaper stated, "We have always thought of America as the land of the bomb, the gadget, and the dollar. Martha Graham has

Appalachian Spring, in Tokyo, with Stuart Hodes.

shown us that America has a soul." Here and in other lands, surprised reporters and editors wondered in print why America had concealed such great assets as Graham and assumed that we were selfish about sharing our great artists with the world. It never occurred to them that politicians and businessmen had been contemptuous of the value of art.

On closing night in Japan the audience set off tiny firecrackers to honor the Graham dancers and wept at their imminent departure. Burma, Thailand, India embraced Martha Graham and her dancers onstage and off. The audiences in India had no doubt that she was the most important visitor America had ever sent them, far more important than ambassadors with planeloads of dollars (and they said just that in print). Dance to them was more than entertainment; it was a statement of culture, even of faith, for in their own ancient Hindu religion it was taught that the world, nay, the universe had been created by Shiva, Lord of Dance, in a divine cosmic dance. Not since Ruth St. Denis, who had come to India with her own tributes to the dance of India thirty years before, had Indians welcomed so warmly an American ambassador.

Asian audiences had no trouble at all understanding Graham dances. What bewildered many Americans—Martha's tormented heroines, her capsuling of time, her rolling or falling onto the floor—bothered the Easterners not one whit. They may never have heard of Medea, but they knew a witch when they saw one; they knew that the gods made time stand still and that the Fates created dramas that were not for mortals to question. And why should dance ceremonies have literal meanings? They themselves had danced certain measures for millennia and did not always know why they did what they did except that they always had. Martha brought to them completely familiar ceremonies of good versus evil, of passions disrupted by fate, of antagonists and protagonists reenacting the eternal conflicts that beset men and gods and, yes, of ancestral footsteps that are not explained but accepted.

For the next twenty years Martha was a favorite of the State Department whenever funds made it possible to send her to Europe or back to the Orient (as they did for a triumphant tour, after her own dancing days were over, in 1974). In 1963, when she was in her seventieth year, she served her country brilliantly in England, where she had the press at her feet at long last, and in western Europe and the Middle East as well.

Only two members of congress still had doubts, and voiced them. They were Edna Kelley of New York and Peter Freylinghuysen of New Jersey. Perhaps in a misguided effort to be sure that government funds were being properly spent on noncontroversial activities, they questioned the propriety of Graham's *Phaedra*. It is a dramatic ballet derived from the ancient Greek drama of the aging stepmother who, during her husband's absence, falls in love with the son, attempts to seduce him, is rejected, and in anger accuses him of trying to seduce her, an accusation that causes the father to kill his own son. The story had also served the classical French theater with Racine's great drama *Phèdre*.

Perhaps the classic was unknown to the two Representatives. At any rate, they found Graham's *Phaedra* shockingly erotic and did not want public monies to be spent on it. Freylinghuysen was upset

about a stage bed in which, he thought, Martha and a
male dancer came together.

In response to his criticism, Martha told an
interviewer in a deceptively mild voice that the bed,
designed by Noguchi, was unbelievably uncomfortable,
that it could hold only one person, and that if the
congressman thought that anything of an amorous
nature could be accomplished in it, he was welcome to
try it out. With the sweetest smile and in a soft voice she
concluded, "I think eroticism is a lovely thing. Don't
you?"

In the 1950s Martha experimented with a new
form of choreography. Long before, she had been a
highly successful exponent of the solo recital. It is a most
difficult form of entertainment, requiring both versatil-
ity and a personality powerful enough to hold the stage
alone. In 1950 and in 1951, on commission from the
Louisville Symphony, she created for herself two symphonic solos. *Judith*, with a score by William Schuman,
was the first. The orchestra was onstage and Graham
performed in front of it. Because the stage depth left
little space for her movement, the choreography was
designed laterally. Martha capitalized on this limitation
by making the strip of stage seem like a pathway along
which the episodes, each more dramatic than the
preceding one, took place, building to a powerful
climax. Her heroine was the biblical Judith, who
murdered a tyrant to save her people. Twelve years
later she did *Legend of Judith*, with a new score by an
Israeli composer.

Martha danced *Judith* for my "Y" series and
explained to the audience its structure and its dramatic
and symbolic elements. Inadvertently, she provided an

interesting clue as to what she thought about while performing. She told her audience that when she danced she submerged her own being in whatever role she was playing. Graham was dismissed, and Judith or Jocasta or the Appalachian Bride or whoever, lived on stage. Then, in discussing performances of *Judith*, she mentioned how difficult it had been to dance this in the downstage area, close to the footlights, at Constitution Hall in Washington, D.C. "There are brass rings there for electrical outlets," she said, "and you wonder if you're going to catch your toe and fall or have some sort of accident." I should have known better, but I countered, "I thought you said you never thought of anything onstage, that you became the character itself." She looked me full in the face: "I do. I looked at those rings and said to myself, 'One more hazard for Judith to face.' "

You can't win with Martha.

The second symphonic solo was *The Triumph of Saint Joan*, with a score by Norman Dello Joio, whose music for *Diversion of Angels* had entranced audiences as much as Martha's choreography. The solo focused upon three aspects of Joan: the Maiden, the Warrior, the Martyr. It was an effective work but not wholly successful, and Martha knew it. Her unsupported solo days were over. She had to think now in terms of a company supporting her as the central figure in a dance work. Indeed, her dancers were extensions of herself. No longer could she carry a Joan alone. She mentioned this to no one, and she didn't wait to be criticized for slowly ebbing powers. She recognized the decline from within before anyone could recognize it from without. Her Puritan fortitude saw her through this transitional period.

Earlier she had successfully rebelled against a different aspect of her Puritan heritage, one that looked down upon the body and considered sex as a near-satanic necessity, which should not be mentioned. She felt that the pelvic area housed the joy of sex, that it was the temple of conception. She related the body's physical, creative process to the artist's creative process. Once she shocked a large group of new students at a college dance class when she asked them to sit on the floor but to do it in sequence so she could watch each one as the movement was made. When they had done what she asked, she simply said, "Thank you." A curious student said, "Miss Graham, why did you ask us to sit and then not give us something to do, some exercise?" Martha replied, "I simply wanted to see which ones of you cherished your genitals. If you crash down to the floor, it means you have no concern for them. And if you are indifferent to your creative areas in a physical sense you will be indifferent to your creative forces in an artistic sense—and you will never become dancers."

In addition to asking that her students cherish their bodies, she demanded that they exert total discipline over these bodies. She insisted that it required ten years of remorseless training to make a professional dancer, and she was probably right. She also could demand the impossible of a body and get what she asked for. As an example, she had in one of her classes a young author-editor, George Zournas, who had no intention of becoming a dancer. He adored Graham and relished using his body in dance experience and exercise. One day, a hot day, he came to class wearing a new pair of blue swim trunks. The studio had just had a new surfacing job done on the floor. It was spotless. George, one of the many students, began to perspire. To his horror, he noted that the blue dye in his trunks was beginning to stain the floor. Martha noticed it also. She said nothing to George directly. She simply looked at her sweating class and said, "I forbid you to perspire. It's only self-indulgence." George later told me, "And I did stop. I was too scared of her to disobey her." Impossible, you say? But true!

The 1950s were a busy decade for Martha. There were the triumphant tours abroad, two symphonic ballets, and a continuously heavy teaching schedule in the handsome house and garden that Bethsabée had bought as a school and studio for Martha and as headquarters for her own B. de Rothschild Foundation. Martha also created other major dances and took part in Bethsabée's "The American Dance" Broadway festival, which brought together the most impressive aggregation of modern dancers ever assembled. Martha, of course, was not a joiner, but she could hardly say "no" to Bethsabée, and her participation was rewarded with a New York season of her own.

The major new creations, in addition to the symphonic dance solos, were *Seraphic Dialogue*, a wholly new version of her *Saint Joan* (with the same score). This interpretation employed three Joans (the Maid, the Warrior, and the Martyr) and a composite Joan, plus the Angel Michael and two attendant angels; a delightful piece called *Canticle for Innocent Comedians*; her own racy and sardonic view of the Garden of Eden, *Embattled Garden*, in which Adam and Eve had to cope not only with the temptations of the serpent but also with those of the seductress Lilith; a ballet collaboration with George Balanchine called *Episodes*, for the New York

City Ballet; and the first evening-length work ever created in the field of modern dance, *Clytemnestra*. Of these, Martha herself danced only in *Episodes* (for a limited number of performances) and in the title role of *Clytemnestra*.

The original idea was that Graham and Balanchine, using the modern music of Anton Webern, would choreograph *Episodes* separately, in two independent parts, but share dancers. Balanchine, in his section, had a solo for Paul Taylor, a Graham dancer, couched in the Graham style, but the remainder of his "episodes" was cast in his own version of modernized ballet and was danced by his own New York City Ballet dancers. Martha chose a dramatic theme, in contrast to Balanchine's abstract dances, for her "episode" and focused upon the conflict between Mary Queen of Scots and Elizabeth I of England. Sallie Wilson of the ballet played Elizabeth and Martha was Mary. The duel between the two women in their struggle for single power was conceived as a tennis match. At the premiere, the Graham work received the loudest and longest applause, and there was little question that the laurels of that particular evening belonged to Martha Graham.

There were backstage repercussions. Martha later told me that neither Balanchine nor Lincoln Kirstein, the company's general director, had come to her dressing room after the ballet to say thank you for the experiment. She felt that even if they disliked what she had done with her episode some sort of post-performance response was a minimum courtesy. A ballet spokesman explained rather feebly that Martha had been "difficult" about one of her costumes. Whatever

In *Episodes*, Graham portrayed Mary, Queen of Scots.

the cause, there was a distinct chill. Eventually, Martha's episode was dropped and the New York City Ballet kept the Balanchine sections in its permanent repertory under the title *Episodes.*

Clytemnestra, with a score for voices and orchestra by the Egyptian composer Halim El-Dabh, settings by Noguchi, and lighting by Jean Rosenthal, proved to be a monumental Graham creation. It was also to be the last new work in which Martha, approaching sixty-five, would summon up her waning powers to dance as close to "full out" as she possibly could. In matters of technique, much was curtailed: the leg didn't kick as high as it once did, the front-slide-split-falls were but echoes of what they had once been, and the turns with leg extended to the back were minimal. But her concentration was great and the impact of her characterization potent. It was a triumph for her, her last true triumph as a dancer, and it took every ounce of strength and willpower and, perhaps, desperation that she had within her.

Clytemnestra is onstage constantly, not always moving, but present with an overpowering intensity. Here again, Martha makes the instant an eternity, for the work is an extension of that moment when Clytemnestra, in Hell, asks why she is damned even in Hell itself, why the most awful sinners of Hell are revolted by her. She receives her answer in episodes that show her inexorable progress from unfaithful wife of a king, to the mistress of a conniver, to a plotter and usurper and murderess. She tries, in Hell, to excuse herself. The king had sacrificed their daughter on the altar of the gods to assure a Greek victory over Troy. She suggests that inexorable fate—the goddess of love, Aphrodite—had

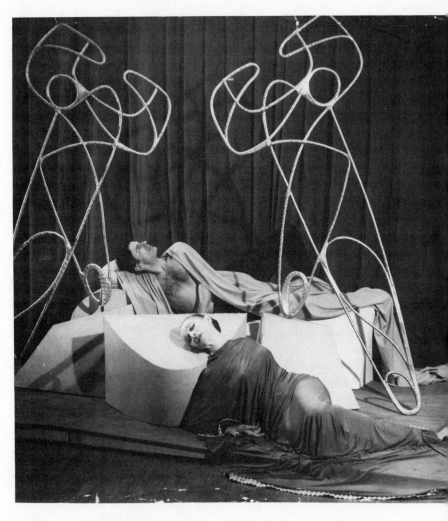

With Bertram Ross in *Clytemnestra*. Setting by Isamu Noguchi.

caused passion to transform Helen of Troy from a creature of beauty into the very cause of the bloody Trojan War. However Clytemnestra looked at the death and destruction lying about her, she could not be blamed. But she knew she was blamed, and restless even among the restless dead, she could find no peace until she admitted her guilt even to the monsters of Hell itself.

Clytemnestra represented a performing (if not a dancing) peak in the Graham career and a choreographic achievement, which, in the same genre of psychological dance-drama, she could never hope to match. The powerful work itself has survived her own retirement as a dancer and has come to be something quite unique in modern dance, good "box office." Despite its length, its depressing theme, even its obscurities, it sells tickets. Since Martha's retirement the title role has been danced, and successfully, by younger Graham dancers, Oriental and black as well as white.

Not all was deep, black tragedy in the Graham repertory. There was a rousing return to comedy, to the sly wit of *Every Soul Is a Circus*, in her later delicious satire on a wife's trials with a boorish husband in *Punch and the Judy*, and in her hilarious *Acrobats of God*, which began to occupy her mind as the decade of the 1950s drew to a close. This would be the first new work of the 1960s, her last decade as a dancer who had electrified audiences around the world for more than fifty years.

Punch and the Judy. From left to right: Jean Erdman, Ethel Butler, Merce Cunningham, Jane Dudley, Erick Hawkins, Graham, David Zellmer, Nina Fonaroff, Pearl Lang, Mark Ryder, David Campbell.

ERIC SCHAAL

Toward the Shadows

It was no secret that Martha was relying somewhat more on alcohol to keep herself going, to dim her awful recognition of the fact that she must soon stop dancing. Drink helped her to fool herself into believing that she could postpone the inevitable. Friends were deeply concerned, her dancers were terrified when she went onstage with less than full control of her faculties, and the gossips spread the news throughout the world of theater.

I spoke to old Louis Horst of my worries. In his calm growl and with that air of inevitability (although not abject acceptance of anything) which came to him as an old man, he said, "I wouldn't worry too much if I were you, Walter." Then he added that when she was in the agonizing—"like birth pains," he said—processes of creating a new work, she would, in moments of frustration and doubt, turn to liquor, but that she never took a drop when she was performing. Perhaps she had followed these rules in Louis's day, but by the 1950s she mixed alcohol and performing. It got worse in the 1960s.

A great deal of it had to do with getting older. She was nearing seventy, and it was impossible for her to dance as she had once danced. After a remarkably successful lecture-demonstration, which she gave with her dancers, one in which her mere presence, her brilliant gestures, and her caressive voice suggested that she could continue to appear onstage forever, I hinted to her that this might be a new performing career for her. "I know what you are thinking about," she said. "But it won't do. I can never be like Miss Ruth. She was always gentle of movement. I've made a reputation as a virtuosic dancer. The public expects it of me. I wouldn't be permitted to change." But the virtuosity was gone.

On one of her late-night calls—and she would talk for hours by phone to those she had known a long time—she suddenly said, "I hate age!"

Gertrude Macy, who produced Graham seasons and tours, told me that she had tried to convince Martha that she did not need to try to dance any longer, that she was a brilliant choreographer, a fabulous teacher, a superb speaker, even a great actress. "And after I'd say all these things to her," Gertrude told me, "she'd say 'I've never been a very good choreographer and I really don't know how to teach. I'm a dancer and that's all I've ever been. Take that away and there's nothing left.' "

There was nothing anyone could do for her. She was simply determined to hang on as long as she could. There was at least one performance of *Clytemnestra* in which she barely hung on. One of her dancers, no longer with her company now, told me that in the first part Martha was moving about with no regard to what she had choreographed. "I think she was dieting and taking reducing pills and she probably had something to drink, but none of us knew what to do onstage or where to go. We tried to adjust to her. It was frightening. The audience probably never guessed because she's so impressive onstage, but we knew. After intermission, she came back cold sober. I don't know what she did in her dressing room. But she was all right for the rest of it."

The choreography of the 1960s started out frantically but with great good humor. *Acrobats of God* was an instant success. Martha herself was in it, but there was nothing difficult in the way of action. She sat or posed a great deal of the time and used her expressive face to its fullest in portraying her character, a choreographer inexorably driven by a Taskmaster with a long whip to go ahead and do her job. As he snapped his whip, she'd get up and start to create for her dancers but not before giving him a withering look, casting her eyes heavenward in a "Get Him!" look of exasperation, and shrugging her shoulders in a "Well, what can you expect of a character like that!"

The dancers satirized classical ballet training, holding the traditional *barre*, or railing, as they did their exercises—but with a wild mirror motif. Martha had some dancers standing on a sort of bridge, while their counterparts, or reflections, were placing their feet on

Acrobats of God.   RON PROTAS

the underside of the bridge and doing their *barre* exercises upside down! The work was filled with all kinds of feats done with great ease, exactitude, and dash by the Graham company. They did indeed seem like acrobats of God.

Oddly enough, Martha had not intended *Acrobats* to be a comedy. It had started out with the idea that dancers had to labor endlessly and unrelentingly to achieve that perfection which would make them "divine athletes," to use Martha's favorite definition of the dancer. She put herself in it as a sort of presiding choreographer-teacher-supervisor because she needed a role and because she too had been subjected to the whip of her conscience. But on opening night the audience laughed at one of the very first measures that Martha performed. She caught on immediately, started clowning for all she was worth, and led her company into a smashing comedy success.

Besides the controversial *Phaedra*, she came up with two winners for the company in which she did not dance. One was *Secular Games*, a playful piece with a softly erotic luster in which there was a vigorous dance for men, a lovely dance for women, and a concluding dance in which the sexes mingled deliciously as they displayed bodies moving with great beauty in a Utopia.

The other dance was *Circe*, based on the myth of the enchantress who lured men to her island home, changed sailors into swine, and captivated the great Ulysses. In effect, it mirrored the irresistible magic of a woman, witch or not. The role was created especially for Mary Hinkson, one of Martha's most brilliant dancers.

After *Phaedra*, in 1962, Martha's own vehicles were

of negligible worth. They did little more than give her an excuse to get onstage. Once there she could only walk or sit or kneel (although getting up from a kneeling position was now presenting difficulties).

Witch of Endor, Cortege of Eagles, A Time of Snow, The Lady of the House of Sleep, dealing with age and sorrow and death, were minimal dance excuses to let the great one perform one more time. They were quickly forgotten, for although some contained traces of the Graham powers of choreography, they were painfully limited, except for the continuing force of her mere presence. Everyone, or almost everyone, was kind. The press and older devotees could not be cruel to one who had done so much for dance for so long. The young were less charitable, sometimes even scathing. What was Martha Graham to them but a legend? When they saw her in the 1960s for the first time, they saw an old woman who could no longer dance. With some justification they wondered what all the shouting was about. We tried to describe what she *used* to do, how thrilling were the kicks, the turns, the swift runs, the monumental falls and slides, the gorgeous face, the hypnotic presence, and we'd say, "You see what we mean, don't you? Isn't it better to see her just stand there than to see almost anyone else move?" They tried to understand, I think, but they had no images, as we did, to summon up and to people the stage in living memory.

Still, the 1960s had their rewarding moments. Martha had major tours of Europe in 1963 and 1967 as well as successful seasons in America. She was honored by receiving the Capezio Dance Award, the most prestigious recognition in the dance profession, and one given not for a specific event but for unmatched service

The Batsheva Dance Company presented works by internationally famous choreographers like Graham, Jerome Robbins, José Limón, as well as by young Israeli choreographers.

to dance in America; university degrees; New York City's Handel Medallion, the city's highest honor for the arts; Martha Graham Day in Santa Barbara, and endless citations, receptions, and testimonials. Even more important, she saw modern dance, and her own brand at that, take root in foreign soil.

The Baroness Bethsabée de Rothschild, an ardent supporter of the new State of Israel, had moved there and was focusing her time, talents, and resources on activities in her new home. She was not able to fund Graham enterprises as generously as she had in the past. But she brought Martha to Israel frequently to perform, to teach, and, most important, to found Israel's first modern dance group, the Batsheva Dance Company. Martha and her assistants trained the new company expertly. Graham works were given to the growing repertory, and when Martha herself could not be present to direct the company, she saw to it that major Graham descendants—Jane Dudley, Norman Walker, Robert Cohan, and others—kept matters on a high professional level. On its first tours, the Batsheva Dance Company earned excellent reviews and was treated by the European and American press as an important dance unit of international stature. In time, the Baroness turned her interest toward a second company, the ballet-oriented Bat-Dor Dance Company, directed by de Rothschild's protégée, Jeanette Ordman, also the company's principal dancer.

In England, Robin Howard carried his enormous admiration for Graham to fruition by helping to finance a program whereby British dancers could come to America and study (tuition-free) at the Graham School in New York. In 1967 he assisted in the establishment of a Graham school and company, the London Contemporary Dance Company, which, under Robert Cohan as director, made its impact felt not only in London but throughout England and on the Continent.

In 1958 Martha had made her first professionally directed and prepared movie. It was called *A Dancer's World*. It is a magnificent documentary on the technique, the performing of dance, particularly Graham dance. Martha does not dance in it. As it opens, she is at the makeup table in a stage dressing room. She starts talking about dance; her voice narrates over the actions of her company. At the end, she rises and goes to the door of the room, heading for the stage, the dancer's world.

In the 1960s she made films of *Appalachian Spring* and *Night Journey*. Her dancers were seen rehearsing or practicing on television, too, but she herself always refused to be seen on that medium. She would allow only her voice to be heard as she described a rehearsal, or she would talk as still photographs of herself and her dancers were shown. Her explanation was very simple: "I'm a vain woman."

Since television is a visual medium, network chiefs and reporters would insist that if she would not appear, they would not provide news coverage of her in conjunction with, say, a Broadway season. Somehow, her press director, Tom Kerrigan, would coax the television stations to send cameras and reporters to the Graham studio with promises of great rehearsal shots and the chance to meet and talk with the fabled lady. Grudgingly, they'd say, "Well, we'll see." Then Martha would charm them into complete submission. Lights and camera would be trained on the young and beautiful Graham dancers, while the reporter, with only a microphone, would kneel beside Martha and ask her questions. Placing a hand on his shoulder, and giving him her most winning smile, she would make him feel that her husky-voiced answers were for him alone. After one such session—whoever heard of anyone being starred on television without being seen?—Kerrigan heaved a sigh of relief: "God! that's just got to be one of the greatest coups in my career as a press agent. Selling a *voice* to television!"

Martha, of course, had always been fussy about photographs, even still photographs. She hated candid shots, especially as she got older, and when she was eighty she would sometimes insist that a reception be cleared of all photographers before she made her entrance. Of all who photographed her as a dancer, none equaled Barbara Morgan, who worked with her at the very peak of her career. The Morgan book of Graham photographs represents one of the great dance documents of the twentieth century.

In that decade of the '60s Martha also made a gesture of peace toward Ted Shawn. He had often asked her to appear on his Sunday lecture series at his summertime Jacob's Pillow Dance Festival, but she would always procrastinate with "if possible." Weidman had danced in the festival and Doris had visited. Suddenly in 1960 Martha said she would go for a lecture-demonstration and picked a date. It happened to be the day on which I had been slated to speak—I lectured at the Pillow once each summer—so I joyfully gave up my time for her appearance. It was just twenty years since I had cajoled Martha into a rapprochement with Ted, Doris, and Charles at Miss Ruth's New York

Martha Graham presents the Capezio Dance Award to
Ruth St. Denis, 1961.

studio. That had been a tense but very correct affair, with everyone embracing everyone else tentatively and posing for a photo for *The New York Times* Sunday section.

At her Jacob's Pillow appearance, Martha was treated with great honor, and Shawn, always given to flowery speeches from the stage, made one think that he and Martha had adored each other since 1916, except for some passing minor misunderstandings. The truth was that they still disliked each other intensely. What Shawn wanted was to add the Graham name to the unequaled roster of international dance stars he had brought to Jacob's Pillow since he had founded it in 1933. Martha, on her part, may have begun to feel a bit nostalgic about the past, although she always protested that forward was her only direction. Also, while gaining an ever-increasing public for her theater of dance, she was losing, and swiftly, the adoration of a new generation of dancers. The new avant-garde was as against her "inner man," "interior landscapes," and her theater-temple filled with its psychological gods and demons as she had been against the exoticism, the romanticism, the eclecticism of Denishawn. Maybe, for a fraction of a moment at Jacob's Pillow, she was looking back on something in the person of Ted Shawn that made her still the avant, and not the rear, "garde."

It was in this decade that she developed her concept of a dance-lecture demonstration into a beautifully choreographed, highly dramatic event with herself as star. She enjoyed the format as long as it did not replace her own dancing. Eventually, of course, it would do just that, and with success. But in the '60s these appearances were an easy, pleasurable, and remunerative sideline for her. For she was always a remarkable speaker. She could speak extemporaneously from her vast knowledge of literature, dance, and theater and her own stupendous array of personal experience. Often, she would make audiences feel that she was coining fabulous phrases on the instant just for them—her timing is as perfect as that of an acrobat or a veteran vaudevillian—when in most cases she was simply dipping into her memory of colorful, unusual quotes from poets or scientists, many obscure or forgotten. The published *Notebooks of Martha Graham* indicate the range of Martha's private world of images.

She danced in public for the last time in 1969. It was not announced as a farewell but she must have known when the final curtain fell on her engagement at the New York City Center. Many of us felt retirement must come soon but we hoped it would be transitional, as she changed from dancer to actress. But she had more than her own troubles weighing upon her.

Her sister Jeordie had been very ill and in and out of hospitals. Martha worried deeply about her. Then Martha herself collapsed. For two years she was often hospitalized herself, convalescing at the country home of friends in Cross River, New York, not much more than an hour from Manhattan. She was under medication and on a diet, forbidden to have any liquor. She never set foot in her own studio for almost a year. She kept in touch with Lee Leatherman, her manager, by telephone, but she expressed little interest in the school and no interest at all in a sort of workshop series, using Graham students, he had set up under the direction of Mary Hinkson and Bertram Ross, Martha's longtime partner after Erick's day. She wouldn't—perhaps she

A lecture at Philharmonic Hall.   DORA SANDERS

couldn't—help launch some sort of a project to keep alive the unique Graham repertory. If she couldn't dance herself, she didn't seem to care what happened to any of her masterpieces.

Several times she was said to be near death. The Graham career seemed to be a thing of the past, and the chief concern was how to keep the Graham school going and to maintain, even through modest studio performances, at least some of the Graham repertory. Attendance at the school had fallen off when it was apparent that there was no company for a student to aim for.

The years 1971 and 1972 seemed to herald the end. There was no income to speak of, but money was the least of Martha's worries. She had never felt concerned about it. She had always shopped extravagantly, planned extravagant productions, given extravagant gifts, and simply assumed that money would somehow materialize to pay her bills. Worst of all now, there seemed to be no hope that Martha would survive either physically or artistically. She had predicted that when dancing was taken away from her, she would be nothing, that it would be all over.

And then a young man entered her life. He worshipped her. He believed in her. He would not permit her to die. In 1973 she was reborn.

Renewal of a Legend

The young man's name was Ron Protas. A law student and a gifted theater photographer, he came into Martha Graham's life by way of his camera. His love of dance and his fascination with celebrities were contributing factors. A good many of his early pictures were fuzzy or dark; they were all performance shots or backstage candids. But all of them were sensitive to his subject. It was as if the man at the shutter was using the instrument for an act of adoration. He focused on the most fascinating of the dance stars: Margot Fonteyn, Rudolf Nureyev, the swiftly rising American ballerina, Cynthia Gregory, and Martha Graham. A silhouette of

Martha perched on a stool became the Graham trademark for programs, posters, even theater marquees.

He was always protective in the release of his
pictures. He would show prints to his famous subjects
and release only those they approved of. Nureyev and
Fonteyn cared about both their body lines as dancers
and their faces as celebrities. Martha cared about how
her face photographed. When I chose his photos for
illustration of my *Saturday Review* pieces or my books,
Ron would spread them out, usually marginless and cut
into all shapes and sizes, from small postcard to display
piece, on my tables and floor. He was tall, slender,
bespectacled, and almost always laughing or joking. He
never seemed to mind being evicted from theaters
because of his cameras. He'd chuckle, leave, and come
back through another door. He was ever polite, always
solicitous. He treated Dame Margot and Martha with
warmth and great respect.

What Martha, nearing eighty, needed, Ron was
able to provide: gallantry, adoration, and an un-
swerving faith in her future. Ted Shawn had prodded
and needled her; Louis Horst had whipped her into
accomplishing what he knew she could achieve; Erick
Hawkins, as the Ringmaster in *Every Soul Is a Circus*, and
in real life as well, used his male authority as the head
of the household and as the chief male in the Graham
company to exert tremendous pressure on her. But at
eighty, as she indicated in her humorous responses to
the Taskmaster with the whip in *Acrobats of God*, she was
beyond all that nonsense. She did not want to be
ordered about any more. She wanted to be cared for.
Ron Protas cared.

With him at her side, Martha made a comeback, a

spectacular one, an unbelievable one. She came to understand that there was something for her in dance even if she herself would never dance again. She was no longer bitter, angry, and defiant about what age had done to her. Rueful, yes, and very sad and regretful, but no longer defeated. She stopped drinking, began to take care of herself, and surprised everyone, including the government of the United States, which sent her on an arduous tour of the Orient in 1974; that she still had untapped wellsprings of energy, incredible stamina, and a fierce strength in her little body was obvious to all.

She marched into her school and restored it to its former prestige. She herself taught almost daily, and students, even veteran Graham followers, were astounded by the wholly new teaching materials and images she brought to her classes. For her classes, in truth, were as inventive as her choreography. Once again, while adhering to her basic principles of movement, she would explore still further the movement possibilities of the body. In one class she might concentrate on arms and provide her students with new arm disciplines and patterns they had never experienced before. Or she might focus upon the upper spine or, in another class, relate the movement of the upper spine to the neck and arms. Her invention, as a teacher, was prodigious.

She was less successful in her return to choreography. Her first works after four years' absence were *Mendicants of Evening* (in which she used an electronic score for the first time) and *Myth of a Voyage* (Martha had done several "voyage" dances over the years, none of them successful). They were not first-rate Graham. The chief problem was that Martha herself could no longer dance and, in the past, most of her successful works had, at their core, her own person. Choreography for her company, not just for herself, grew out of her own movement experiences.

There was plenty to do, however, for a repertory of Graham masterworks needed to be restored and returned to the stage. A few years earlier she had resented younger dancers taking over her own roles, and often the pieces got onstage with little help or none at all from her. Mary Hinkson or Pearl Lang had been forced to take on such responsibilities. Now, with her recovery, Martha took charge. For the first time she assumed responsibility. And because she possessed, as do many of us, a need for some proof of our own immortality—a sense that whatever we have done won't just disappear —she came to admit to herself that her own immortality was not in her own body but in that body of dances which she had given to the world. In *Dark Meadow* she had treated immortality as the "ancestral footsteps" that echo a future. In her new *Mendicants*, which included spoken lines from the poems of the twentieth-century French writer St. John Perse, she had accepted "great age" because it represented "a road of glowing embers, not of ash."

The 1973 Broadway season, her first in four years, at the Alvin Theater was a triumph in every way. Joining her dancers in a curtain call at the close of opening night, Martha received a standing ovation as she made a new pact of service with her public. For this season, she relied on Mary Hinkson and Bertram Ross and some of her other veteran dancers. Mary, especially, served her brilliantly in many roles, including *Clytemnestra*.

But trouble was brewing. Ron was usurping the authority of these veterans. Even old friends seemed to have to reach her through Ron, and it was he who could grant permission or refuse it. He was her new company administrator and because he had willingly assumed many of her burdens and her problems, she usually permitted him to have his way. Neither a dancer, a choreographer, nor an administrator, he was not immediately prepared for the responsibilities.

Mary Hinkson and Bert Ross left the company. Debts had long since piled up. Serious problems confronted the company's board of directors. Whatever his troubles with the business and administrative sides (although he quickly proved to be a good fund raiser), no one could question how essential Ron Protas was to Martha Graham. He had brought her back from the limbo of her despair.

In 1974 the difficulties were cleared away. There was a new chairman of the board, Francis Mason. As the U.S. cultural attaché at the Court of St. James's, he had aided Martha in her London and Edinburgh seasons.

Not new to the company but new to major roles were some of the younger members of the Graham troupe. Takako Asakawa, Yuriko Kimura, Ross Parkes, Tim Wengerd, Phyllis Gutelius, and David Hatch Walker were brilliant in their new assignments. With their rise, something happened to the Graham repertory. These young dancers were not *repeating* old roles, they were *renewing* them. Martha, while guiding them, gave them free rein, even encouraged them to try new departures in interpretation.

Where her dances, a few years before, had seemed

dated to the new, critical, and searching avant-garde in
dance, they now claimed attention and respect, mainly
because an equally young dance generation was inter-
preting them differently. Martha Graham returned,
then, not simply as a legend, but in the very lead of the
avant-garde. To most, she was still far ahead of her
dissident dancing children.

Once more, the U.S. Department of State knew
that in Martha Graham they had an exportable
product of great worth. With her eightieth birthday
behind her, she set out on an arduous tour of the Orient
with her company. She was in the theater every night;
she taught; she coached; she spoke in public and in
private. She met presidents and monarchs, aristocrats
and working people. She treated all with her gracious-
ness and those lovely, poetic words that the Oriental
adores.

To the Japanese she said, "To be in Japan again is
like having a lovely dream become real. Japan with its
intrinsic love of beauty and infallible sense of proportion
and its excitement is a challenge to the world. What
Japan has done as a nation, as a people, to make
apparent the natural forces of life that surround us is a
treasured gift to humanity throughout the world. A
single brushstroke with its vision and its discipline and
its urgency has added a new dimension to the history of
art and to dance; its intensity of expression, its economy
of apparent effort, and its sense of mystery is a constant
wonder and delight. I return to Japan as I would
approach a stream of living water."

For Martha, life began again at eighty. Her New
York season was a smash, the tour of the Far East a
triumph, an autumn tour of the United States a roaring

success. Martha herself participated in a limited number of programs in her brilliant lecture-demonstrations, now part of the Graham repertory. Honors were heaped upon her by such institutions as the New York Public Library and the Cathedral of St. John the Divine, where she spoke from the pulpit.

Rudolf Nureyev, the ballet star, haunted her performances in New York whenever he had evenings or matinees free from his performing schedules, and Martha, reciprocating, visited his performances as he danced with Britain's Royal Ballet or the National Ballet of Canada. Martha, who once denounced ballet, created for Nureyev, as he wanted her to. Dame Margot Fonteyn was looking for new directions, away from Swan Queens and teen-age Juliets. She looked toward Martha, and Martha, with eagerness, welcomed the great ballerina choreographically with *Lucifer*, made expressly for Fonteyn and Nureyev.

The future was what mattered; Martha's voyage was not yet completed. Did that voyage begin on the good ship *Mayflower* when it brought her ancestors to the New World, or did the voyage begin much later when a great-grandfather, traveling in steerage, came to a new land? Or does the journey go back to those ancestral footsteps, made before the dawn of time, which gave Martha the pulse and beat for *Dark Meadow*?

To Martha, life was a voyage. She had used that word in the titles of some of her dances. She used "errand" too, and *Deaths and Entrances* (the title of her dark and deep explorations of the tormented spirit of the Brontë sisters), and *Transitions*, and *Course*, and, of course, "journey."

What drove her on to continue these journeys,

The 1975 Capezio Dance Award is presented to Robert Irving (left), musical director and principal conductor of the New York City Ballet, by Martha Graham, as Walter Terry looks on.

voyages, errands? In 1974 she said to me, "I have a feeling that everyone is terribly lonely. And aloneness is one of our reasons for fearing death. The thing I feel with an audience is that I'm not alone. Whether they like me or don't like me at least they are positive. I'd rather they didn't like me than that they were apathetic.

"But however much people may help you, you are still a Viking on a ship going out to sea alone for the last time when you are in the lonely and agonizing process of creating a new work. At least every time you create a new dance it seems that this must be the last voyage. But you must make it, you must. I think perhaps this voyage, this errand, is actually the search for tranquility. . . . I guess it might even be the search for happiness."

On her own restless quest she traveled the world with her own unique theater of dance. She hoped that it would be truly a "global theater," for as she herself said, "the emotions, the inclinations, the violences are common to all people. And I would hope that something of this time, of what I have done in this time, would go into the mainstream and would enrich dancing."

Then, she added, "Each of us is unique and if you don't fulfill that uniqueness in whatever course your life may take, in whatever position you may hold, it is lost for all time. It is man's privilege and terror and job to reveal himself, to BE himself."

Martha had been unique—and that means alone within herself—for more than eighty years. Unlike most of us she fulfilled that uniqueness, for if the avant-garde composer Edgard Varèse was right in his belief that "everyone is born with genius but some keep it only a

56Renewal of a Legend

minute," then it can be said of Martha Graham that
she kept her uniqueness, her genius going on voyage
after voyage, errand after errand, journey after journey
for a lifetime.

That Martha Graham passed through eighty years
is of no particular importance in itself. We may look at
it as phenomenal, as a dramatic act of survival, or as a
"unique" example of a woman who chose to press
onward when she had earned the right to sit down, to
lie down, or, even, to die peacefully. But Martha cannot
be measured by ordinary standards. I find her in this
line from St. John Perse's *Chroniques*, which she used in
Mendicants of Evening:

"Divine turbulence, be ours to its last eddy. . . ."

The voyage continues.

RON PROTAS

Choreographic Chronology

Over the years, Martha Graham has created almost two hundred dances. The following is a list of some of the most important, either solos or company works. The date and place given are those of the first performance. Where costume credits are not listed, the designer is Martha Graham. Among several lighting designers, the principal one was Miss Graham's favorite, Jean Rosenthal, now deceased.

CHORALE. Music: César Franck. New York, April 18, 1926.

Also the first dance on the first full-length program given by Martha Graham.

REVOLT. Music: Arthur Honegger. New York, October 16, 1927.

The first major dance of "social comment," it came to characterize the "cult of ugliness" in the newly emerging "modern dance." Satirized by the Broadway comedienne Fanny Brice in a takeoff called "Rewolt."

IMMIGRANT. Music: Josip Slavenski. New York, April 22, 1928.

Another dance of social comment. This one was in two sections: Steerage, Strike.

FOUR INSINCERITIES. Music: Sergei Prokofiev. New York, January 20, 1929.

The four themes are Petulance, Remorse, Politeness, Vivacity.

LAMENTATION. Music: Zoltán Kodály. New York, January 8, 1930.

One of Graham's most famous solo dances, one which represents her distilling of an emotional experience into an essence. This is not a lamenting of a specific tragedy but a synthesis of all lamentations for all sorrows.

PRIMITIVE MYSTERIES. Music: Louis Horst. New York, February 2, 1931.

A dance for Graham and a company of girls, a landmark in the Graham career. A stark, spare but beautiful distillation of all those rituals—prehistoric, historic, or contemporary—by which primitive people make supplication, sacrifice, and praise to their gods. The dance is divided into Hymn to the Virgin, Crucifixus, Hosanna.

AMERICAN PROVINCIALS. Music: Louis Horst. New York, November 11, 1934.
Her first major dance dealing with her own American ancestral heritage. A dance in two parts: Act of Piety, Act of Judgment.

FRONTIER. Music: Louis Horst; décor: Isamu Noguchi. New York, April 28, 1935.
The dance is subtitled "An American Perspective of the Plains." It was the first Graham dance to use décor. It became Graham's most celebrated solo. Like *Lamentation*, it is a dance of "essence," for no specific (in time or place) frontier is actually depicted. Rather, the dancer suggests the meaningfulness of the word itself.

CHRONICLE. Music: Wallingford Riegger; décor: Isamu Noguchi. New York, December 20, 1936.
A long and not wholly successful comment on the tragedy of the Spanish Civil War. An example of one of Graham's rare excursions into political commentary in dance.

DEEP SONG. Music: Henry Cowell. New York, December 19, 1937.
A much more successful dance about the Spanish Civil War, this time focusing upon the personal tragedy of a woman in wartime.

AMERICAN DOCUMENT. Music: Ray Green; settings: Arch Lauterer; costumes: Edythe Gilfond. Bennington, Vermont, August 6, 1938.
A major work of Americana, using narration as well as dance movement. The first Graham creation to use a male dancer (Erick Hawkins).

EVERY SOUL IS A CIRCUS. Music: Paul Nordoff; settings: Philip Stapp; costumes: Edythe Gilfond. New York, December 27, 1939.

Although Graham had touched upon comic elements before, this was her first all-comedy success.

EL PENITENTE. Music: Louis Horst; décor: Arch Lauterer; costumes: Edythe Gilfond. Bennington, Vermont, August 11, 1940.

A dance for three. Suggested by an Indian ceremony of the Southwest in which there is a simulated crucifixion in commemoration of the Crucifixion of Jesus. The sect itself is known as the Penitentes.

LETTER TO THE WORLD. Music: Hunter Johnson; settings: Arch Lauterer; costumes: Edythe Gilfond. Bennington, Vermont, August 11, 1940.

One of the most famous and popular of the Graham creations. Based on the life (inner as well as outer) of the New England poetess Emily Dickinson.

DEATHS AND ENTRANCES. Music: Hunter Johnson; settings: Arch Lauterer; costumes: Edythe Gilfond. New York, December 26, 1943.

One of Graham's most profound, "dark," and psychologically motivated dance-dramas. Based on the passions (seen and concealed) of the three famous Brontë sisters.

APPALACHIAN SPRING. Music: Aaron Copland; décor: Isamu Noguchi; costumes: Edythe Gilfond. Washington, D.C., December 30, 1944.

The most famous and most popular of all of

Martha Graham's creations. A tribute to pioneering America and to the Appalachian area where Graham's forebears settled.

DARK MEADOW. Music: Carlos Chávez; décor: Isamu Noguchi; costumes: Edythe Gilfond. New York, January 23, 1946.
A ritual-style dance suggesting a synthesis of ceremonials (from all eras and all cultures) through which man seeks for proof of his own immortality.

CAVE OF THE HEART. Music: Samuel Barber; décor: Isamu Noguchi. New York, May 10, 1946.
The work was originally called *The Serpent Heart.* The central figure is modeled after the classical Medea, who poisoned her rival and killed her own children out of jealousy and vengeance.

ERRAND INTO THE MAZE. Music: Gian Carlo Menotti; décor: Isamu Noguchi. New York, February 28, 1947.
The inspiration is the story of the classical monster, the Minotaur, and the Labyrinth in which he lived and devoured humans sacrificed to him. The Graham version is one's own journey into the human heart to do battle with the element of fear.

NIGHT JOURNEY. Music: William Schuman; décor: Isamu Noguchi. Cambridge, Massachusetts, May 3, 1947.
Suggested by the Greek tragedy of Jocasta who, unknowingly, married her own son and bore him children. The entire dance-drama takes place in that instant when Jocasta learns of her crime.

DIVERSION OF ANGELS. Music: Norman Dello Joio; décor: Isamu Noguchi (not used after the first performance). New London, Connecticut, August 13, 1948.

A dance without plot and the first major work in which Graham herself never performed. A joyous, popular piece and one of the few Graham creations she has permitted to be performed by companies other than her own.

JUDITH. Music: William Schuman. Louisville, Kentucky, January 4, 1950.

Graham's first symphonic solo, danced onstage in front of an onstage orchestra. Later danced in New York, in the new Berlin Concert Hall (1957), and elsewhere. Based on the biblical heroine. (See *Legend of Judith* listing.)

THE TRIUMPH OF SAINT JOAN. Music: Norman Dello Joio. Louisville, Kentucky, December 5, 1951.

A second symphonic solo for Graham based on three aspects of Joan of Arc: Maiden, Warrior, Martyr. (See *Seraphic Dialogue* listing.)

CANTICLE FOR INNOCENT COMEDIANS. Music: Thomas Ribbink; décor: Frederick Kiesler. New York, April 22, 1952.

Not a comedy but a generally joyous work somewhat in the mood of *Diversion of Angels* but different in pattern; for example, in one scene there is a curved blue panel, six or seven feet high and three or four feet wide, that a male dancer presses his body against in various attitudes, as if he were climbing the sky, resting on it, swimming in it, or sliding down it.

SERAPHIC DIALOGUE. Music: Norman Dello Joio; décor: Isamu Noguchi. New York, May 8, 1955. A wholly new version of the Joan of Arc theme, using the same score. In this, three different dancers play the Maiden, the Warrior, the Martyr. And there is a fourth Joan who is a synthesis of the three aspects of the woman. There are angels, too, and St. Michael, who inducts Joan into sainthood. Perhaps this is Graham's most ecstatic (spiritually) and luminous work.

CLYTEMNESTRA. Music: Halim El-Dabh; décor: Isamu Noguchi. New York, April 1, 1958. This is the first program-length work created in the field of modern dance. Basically, it is four acts, but the sections are designated as Prologue, Act I, Act II, Epilogue. Its central figure is Clytemnestra, the classical Greek heroine-murderess, "damned" even among the damned of Hell.

EMBATTLED GARDEN. Music: Carlos Surinach; décor: Isamu Noguchi. New York, April 3, 1958. Graham's sensual, satiric treatment of the Garden of Eden story. There are four characters in what she has described as "a play"—besides Adam and Eve there is the Stranger (who is the Serpent or Satan himself) and Lilith, a temptress for both Satan and Adam.

EPISODES: PART I. Music: Anton von Webern; décor: David Hays; costumes: Karinska. New York, May 14, 1959. An unprecedented collaboration between the most famous classical ballet choreographer of the era,

George Balanchine, and the foremost modern
dance choreographer, Martha Graham. Graham
choreographed Part I, a drama based on the
conflict between Mary Queen of Scots and Queen
Elizabeth I of England. The battle between the
two queens was conceived in terms of a stylized
tennis match, with golden rackets. Graham was
Mary and Sallie Wilson, from the ballet, was
Elizabeth. Part II was all-Balanchine choreography except for a solo designed by Balanchine in
conjunction with Paul Taylor and danced by
Taylor. It was produced by Balanchine's New
York City Ballet. The Balanchine troupe, in later
seasons, has continued to perform only Part II
(minus the Taylor solo).

ACROBATS OF GOD. Music: Carlos Surinach; décor:
Isamu Noguchi. New York, April 27, 1960.
A comedy in which a Taskmaster with a whip
demands that the Choreographer (a role acted by
Graham) and the Dancers (the acrobats of God)
get to work and produce!

ALCESTIS. Music: Vivian Fine; décor: Isamu Noguchi.
New York, April 29, 1960.
A dance based on a classical Greek drama, another
in Graham's "Greek" cycle.

PHAEDRA. Music: Robert Starer: décor: Isamu Noguchi. New York, March 4, 1962.
The classical Greek heroine who falls in love with
her stepson, is rejected by him, and accuses him to
his father of attempted seduction, thus launching a
series of disasters and death.

SECULAR GAMES. Music: Robert Starer; décor: Jean
Rosenthal. New London, Connecticut, August 17,
1962.
A non-narrative, joyous dance involving a virile
dance for men, a lyrical dance for women, and a
playful dance for both sexes.

LEGEND OF JUDITH. Music: Mordecai Seter; décor:
Dani Karavan. Tel Aviv, Israel, October 25, 1962.
A new version (see *Judith*) for full company of an
earlier solo, but with a new score and new setting.

CIRCE. Music: Alan Hovhaness; décor: Isamu Noguchi.
London, September 6, 1963.
A work based on the Greek myth of Circe, the
enchantress.

MENDICANTS OF EVENING. Music: David Walker;
décor: Fangor; text: passages from St. John Perse's
"Chronique." New York, May 2, 1973. (Revised
1974 under title *Chronique.*)
The first work created following Graham's retirement as a dancer in 1969, and choreographed as
she entered her eightieth year. The dance, composed of reflections on old age, contains four major
duets, sensuous and sometimes sensual. In the first
staging an actress (Marian Seldes) performed onstage and spoke the Perse lines; in a later staging
the voice was an offstage one. A recurrent line is
"Great age, behold us." A concluding passage is
"Divine turbulence, be ours to its last eddy."

LUCIFER. Music: Halim El-Dabh; décor: Leandro
Locsin; costumes: Halston; jewelry: Elsa Peretti;
lighting: Ronald Bates. New York, June 19, 1975.

Bibliography

BY MARTHA GRAHAM:

The Notebooks of Martha Graham. New York: Harcourt Brace Jovanovich, 1973.

"The Future of the Dance," *Dance*, April 1939.

"The Audacity of Performance," *Dance Magazine*, May 1953.

"Martha Graham Speaks," *Dance Observer*, April 1963.

"Martha Graham Talks to Dance and Dancers," *Dance and Dancers*, 1963.

ABOUT MARTHA GRAHAM AND THE DANCE:

Armitage, Merle, *Martha Graham*. New York: Dance Horizons, 1968.

Cohen, Selma Jeanne, *Doris Humphrey: An Artist First*. Middletown, Conn.: Wesleyan University Press, 1973.

De Mille, Agnes, *The Book of the Dance.* New York: Golden Press, 1963.

Denby, Edwin, *Looking at the Dance.* New York: Curtis Books, 1973.

Leatherman, LeRoy (text), Swope, Martha (photographs), *Martha Graham: Portrait of the Lady as an Artist.* New York: Alfred A. Knopf, 1966.

Lloyd, Margaret, *The Borzoi Book of Modern Dance.* New York: Alfred A. Knopf, 1949. (Paperback, Dance Horizons, 1960.)

Martin, John, *America Dancing.* New York: Dance Horizons, 1968.

McDonagh, Don, *Martha Graham: A Biography.* New York: Praeger, 1973.

Moore, Lillian, *Artists of the Dance.* New York: Dance Horizons, 1969.

Morgan, Barbara, *Martha Graham: Sixteen Dances in Photography.* New York: Duell, Sloan and Pearce, 1941.

St. Denis, Ruth, *Ruth St. Denis: An Unfinished Life.* New York: Harper & Brothers, 1939. (Paperback, Dance Horizons, 1971.)

Schlundt, Christena, *The Professional Appearances of Ruth St. Denis and Ted Shawn.* New York: The New York Public Library, 1962.

Shawn, Ted (with Gray Poole), *One Thousand and One Night Stands.* New York: Doubleday, 1960.

Terry, Walter, *The Dance in America.* New York: Harper & Row, 1971.

(Further reference materials, available in libraries, include articles in a worldwide selection of newspapers, magazines, encyclopedias, oral tapes, and a few movies such as the documentary *A Dancer's World.*)

Index

About the Author

Walter Terry's first interview as a young newspaperman was with the already-legendary Martha Graham. That was in 1936, and in the years since then his writings and lectures have played an important part in introducing American audiences to the exciting world of contemporary dance. He began his career as dance critic for the Boston *Herald*, was for many years critic and editor on the New York *Herald Tribune*, and is now an editor of the *Saturday Review*. Mr. Terry is the author of more than a dozen books on various aspects of the dance, including biographies of Isadora Duncan and Ruth St. Denis, a frequent lecturer at colleges and universities all over the country, and a script writer, consultant, and commentator for many all-dance presentations on television.